THE HI
SECRETS AND
STORIES OF
WALT DISNEY
WORLD

DISCOVER
THE MAGIC!
MIKE
FOX

MIKE FOX

Copyright © 2016 Mike Fox

All rights reserved.

No part of this publication may be reproduced, distributed, linked to or transmitted in any form or by any means, including photocopying, recording or other electronic or mechanical methods, without the prior written permission of the publisher, except for brief quotations embodied in critical reviews and certain noncommercial uses permitted by copyright law.

No part of this publication, including the photos, may be made available for downloading online or elsewhere without the permission of Mike Fox Publications.

Although every precaution has been taken to verify the accuracy of the information contained herein, no responsibility is assumed for any errors or omissions, and no liability is assumed for damages that may result from the use of this information.

Mike Fox is not associated with the Walt Disney Company

ISBN 10: 0692563512
ISBN-13: 978-0692563519

P - CS - 011517

To my wife, Kristy, and my two children, Brian and Megan. Let's all meet in our dreams by the popcorn cart in the Town Square.

THE HIDDEN SECRETS
& STORIES OF
WALT DISNEY WORLD

"It's hard to teach an old mouse new tricks...but this book provides hours of surprises for the most knowledgeable of Disney fans." – Peter Whitehead – **Walt Disney Hometown Museum**

Includes Secrets and Photos Not Found in Any Other Disney Books, Articles or Web Sites

- The amazing story of how one lucky guest was called upon by Disney to help create an attraction – Published here for the first time

- The message being sent in the telegraph scene of Spaceship Earth – Revealed for the very first time ever

- Where to find 100 Hidden Mickeys in one place

- The first-ever revealed connection between the colorful Mutoscopes of Main Street, U.S.A and a young 12 year-old Walt Disney

- How do the gas street lamps on Main Street, U.S.A. tie to an important event in American history? – Told here for the first time

- The ominous warning at the entrance to the Haunted Mansion which 99% of guests miss

- The never-before-published story of the Imagineers' Frontierland tribute to A.C. Dietz...who lived 100 years before Disneyland

- Where to find the smallest Hidden Mickey in all of Walt Disney World Resort

- How to pilot the Liberty Belle riverboat and receive your own unique pilot's license souvenir

- And many, many more! Over 300 magical secrets arranged as a fun tour throughout the parks. **Complete with photos!**

FOLLOW
DISNEY-SECRETS ONLINE

On the Web:
www.Disney-Secrets.com

On Twitter:
@149G22

On Facebook:
www.Facebook.com/Disney-Secrets
(Look for the icon above)

CONTENTS

INTRODUCTION

Walt Disney World is a grand stage upon which a story of magic, fantasy and enchantment plays out for guests from around the world each and every day. Cast Members perform, attractions entertain, parades delight and fireworks bedazzle as guests young and old watch with wide-eyed wonder and amazement while the story unfolds all around them. But unknown to many, separate and oftentimes whimsical hidden stories play out right alongside the main act, and these stories make up *The Hidden Secrets & Stories of Walt Disney World.*

With your first visits to the parks, it's all about the attractions...as it should be. There are pirate ships to sail, characters to meet, nations to wander, and a tower of terror to explore. But just beyond that is an all new world of discovery...one which the Disney Imagineers have purposely hidden with the hopes you'll find it.

Want to pilot the grand Liberty Square riverboat? All you have to do is ask. That small non-descript sign for coal oil lamps attached to the General Store in Frontierland, which nobody notices? It actually ties not only to Walt's grandfather, but to Walt himself. That wall of countless animal faces in Disney's Animal Kingdom? Look closer and you'll see it holds over 100 small Hidden Mickeys. And that ancient water basin in the China pavilion? You can make its water dance into the air just by rubbing its handles.

And it all came to be with perhaps Walt Disney World's biggest secret of all, it's beginning...

THE BEGINNING OF WALT DISNEY WORLD

"Believe me, it's the most exciting and challenging assignment we have ever tackled at Walt Disney Productions."

Walt Disney speaking about Walt Disney World

THE BEGINNING

The history of Walt Disney World reads like a suspense novel; an exciting story of intrigue, mystery, false identities and real estate deals cloaked in secrecy, but it's also a story of vision, hope, promise and great success.

Walt Disney World Resort was born out of Walt Disney's dream to bring the magic of Disneyland to more guests from around the world and to realize his vision to create a Community of Tomorrow, a harmonious city which embraced the environment, technology and American values which Walt treasured so much.

While dedicated on October 1, 1971, Walt Disney World actually began in 1958 with Walt's commission of Economics Research Associates to study and recommend a location on the East Coast which would allow him to duplicate the success of Disneyland and realize his dream of creating a Community of Tomorrow. Walt was very clear on the criteria for the site . . . it had to have sunny and warm weather year-round, it had to be readily accessible by millions of guests and, perhaps most importantly, it had to have plenty of inexpensive land available for purchase so Walt could protect his new park from the same kind of urban blight that had come to encroach upon Disneyland.

While Disneyland was very successful at bringing magic and memories to the lives of millions of guests and their families, Walt had always been disappointed by how developers and promoters had ringed the park with a tawdry collection of hotels, restaurants and other businesses concerned more about revenue than creating a magical guest experience. With plenty of acreage at his new site, Walt could control the guest experience outside the parks and maintain the magic of his new Disneyland.

In 1959 Palm Beach, Florida was recommended for the new Disney World park over other sites, including Niagara Falls, St. Louis and a site between Washington D.C. and Baltimore. Unfortunately, negotiations over 12,000 acres in North Palm Beach fell through, and a second survey was commissioned to find an alternate site. This suited Walt as he felt the Palm Beach site, while located near water, was subject to humid weather and the full force of hurricanes. Walt declared his desire to have the park be located inland and two other sites were recommended; Ocala and Orlando.

In November of 1963, Walt flew to Florida with Joe Potter, Buzz Price, Jack Sayers, Donn Tatum and Card Walker to make a final decision on the new park's specific location. After flying over the coastline, as well as the swamps and forests of central Florida, Walt returned home with his final decision. The new Disneyland and City of Tomorrow was to be located in central Florida near Orlando.

A MAGICAL SECRET

With Walt's decision, plans were put into high gear and a strategy was developed to make sure Walt could secure enough property for his new park and Community of Tomorrow. It was important to keep word of his decision and their land purchases secret, for if anyone knew Walt Disney was buying land to create a new Disneyland near Orlando, the price per acre would skyrocket overnight. The key now was to buy all the land, over 27,000 acres, without arousing suspicion.

In February of 1964, after a final review by Roy Disney, Walt gave the go ahead to begin acquiring land. Operating under such company names as Reedy Creek Ranch Corporation, Bay Lake Properties, Latin-America Development and Management Corporation and other mysterious names, Walt Disney began buying thousands of acres of land.

In time, word of major land buys began to filter through the community and rumors began to fly. Many believed a large company was looking to build a major manufacturing or headquarter site, and, given the site's proximity to Cape Canaveral and the Kennedy Space Center, speculation focused heavily on aerospace companies, including Boeing, McDonnell Aircraft, Douglas Aviation, Lockheed and others. In addition, companies including Ford, Volkswagen, Chrysler and even Howard Hughes were considered as candidates. Interestingly, some even suspected Walt Disney was buying property for an "East Coast Disneyland."

In October of 1965, after a long and tedious process, Walt had purchased nearly all the land he needed and more . . . 27,258 acres at a price of a little over $5,000,000. More and more people were now convinced it was Walt Disney who was buying the land, and on October 24th, the Orlando Sentinel, as a result of the work of Reporter Emily Bavar, reported in a headline, "We Say It's Disney." With that, Walt made the decision to announce his plans for Florida. On November 15th, 1965, Florida's Governor, Haydon Burns, introduced Walt Disney at a press conference as, "the man of the decade, who will bring a new world of entertainment, pleasure and economic development to the State of Florida."

Walt explained to all those present . . . *"This is the biggest thing we've ever tackled. I might, for the benefit of the press, explain that my brother and I have been together in our business for forty-two years now. He's my big brother, and he's the one that when I was a little fellow I used to go to with some of my wild ideas, and he'd either straighten me out or put me on the right path - or if he didn't agree with me, I'd work on it for years until I got him to agree with me. But I must say that we've had our problems that way, and that's been the proper balance* that we've been needing in our organization . . . In this project, I'd just like to say that I didn't have to work very hard on him. He was with me from the start. Now whether that's good or bad, I don't know."

"I would like to be part of building a model community, a City of Tomorrow, you might say, because I don't believe in going out to this extreme blue-sky stuff that some architects do. I believe that people still want to live like human beings. There's a lot of things that could be done. I'm not against the automobile, but I just feel that the automobile has moved into communities too much. I feel that you can design so that the automobile is there, but still put people back as pedestrians again, you see. I'd love to work on a project like that. Also, I mean, in the way of schools, facilities for the community, community entertainments and life. I'd love to be part of building up a school of tomorrow . . . This might become a pilot operation for the teaching age - to go out across the country and across the world. The great problem of today is the one of teaching."

THE WORLD BEGINS

Walt felt that the tested concepts and technologies of Disneyland had proven very successful, and the success in Anaheim would readily translate to Florida. As a result, he wanted to focus his attention on his new Community of Tomorrow. "The most exciting, and by far the most important part of our Florida project. In fact, the heart of everything we'll be doing in Disney World – will be our Experimental Prototype Community of Tomorrow. We call it EPCOT. EPCOT will take its cues from the new ideas and new technologies that are now emerging from the creative centers of American industry. It will be a community of tomorrow that will never be completed, but will always be introducing and demonstrating and testing new materials and new systems. And EPCOT will always be a showcase to the world for the ingenuity and imagination of American free enterprise."

Walt formed a committee to oversee the planning for what was to become Disney World. Consisting of himself, Marvin Davis and Joe Potter, the planning committee was set up under WED Enterprises, an organization Walt had created in 1952 to oversee the development and construction of Disneyland. In short order, this team and others pushed forward with engineering and design analysis, site preparation plans, infrastructure planning, project PR and even legislative proposals to establish the authority of the Reedy Creek Improvement District as a quasi-governmental entity to oversee this new city and two new municipalities.

Over the ensuing months, Walt threw himself into the Florida project with his creative enthusiasm and visionary genius, with extra attention being paid to his Community of Tomorrow. Sadly, however, Walt's health took a turn for the worse, and on December 15, 1966, a little over one year after announcing his plans for Disney World and Epcot, Walt Disney passed away.

With the passing of Walt Disney, Roy Disney, at the age of 73, put aside his retirement plans and took the lead in developing Disney World, and in the fall of 1967, site preparation began. As a tribute to his brother, Roy declared that the official name of the Florida project would now be recognized as Walt Disney World. *"Everybody knows the Ford car, but not everybody knows it was Henry Ford who started it all. It's going to be Walt Disney World, so people will always know this was Walt's dream."*

Because swampland and forests were chosen as the site of Walt Disney World, one of the first projects was to drain and control the swampland for construction without seriously impacting the area's fragile ecosystem, something which was very important to Walt Disney. To achieve this, 55 miles of canals and levees were constructed along natural contour lines to efficiently control the delicate natural water systems and preserve the environment.

CONSTRUCTING WALT DISNEY WORLD

The construction of Walt Disney World was designed to occur in phases. Phase One focused on providing the key initial vacation amenities required to open the park and provide guests with the Disney experience they had come to expect, including the Magic Kingdom, five resort hotels, golfing and other activities and necessary park infrastructure.

Walt's first choice for the new Magic Kingdom was directly west of Bay Lake, the largest natural body of water on the property. However, tests showed that the land at this site was unsuitable for construction, so the decision was made to excavate this area and fill it with water, thus creating a new body of water, known as the Seven Seas Lagoon. Today, the Seven Seas Lagoon provides a stunning transition for guests as they journey to and from The Magic Kingdom via boat or monorail, thus achieving Walt's desire to maintain the magic well beyond the gates of his new park.

One of the first construction objectives was to raise the height of the land for the new Magic Kingdom by 14 feet. Walt desired to have not only the park itself, but also its main focal point, Cinderella Castle, sit higher than the surrounding property to give it a sense of visual presence. In addition, raising the park was necessary in order to include the "utilidors" and service infrastructure underneath the park, which allowed cast members and service crews to move from location to location within the park without being visible to the guests "on stage." This was borne of Walt's frustration at seeing a Disneyland cast member in western attire walking through Tomorrowland one day while on his way from costuming to his work station. Walt felt this visual conflict of appearance confused guests and detracted from the guests' experience and the magic of Disneyland. From this, Walt came up with the idea of building utility corridors, or utilidors, under the Magic Kingdom, which would allow cast members to move about unseen by guests, as well as provide a means to move trash, water, laundry, etc. all out of view.

With much of the below ground infrastructure completed, construction of the Magic Kingdom began in late 1969, starting with Main Street, U.S.A. and Cinderella Castle. While Imagineers could draw upon Disneyland's Main Street, U.S.A. for both inspiration and direction, the construction of a large 189 foot high castle which captured the magic of a classic Disney animated feature was entirely new for them. Drawing inspiration from Disney Legend Herbert Ryman's work in designing the castle, as well as from the animated feature Cinderella and several real-life French castles, including Chateau de Chambord, Chateau de Chenonceau and Chateau d'Usse, Imagineers completed this work of art and architecture in July of 1971, only three months before the park opened.

On October 1, 1971, Roy Disney opened Walt Disney World and The Magic Kingdom to the delight of countless millions around the world, both young and old. The park's inauguration included Roy's moving dedication, which can be found today on a bronze plaque on Main Street, U.S.A.:

"Walt Disney World is a tribute to the philosophy and life of Walter Elias Disney . . . and to the talents, the dedication, and the loyalty of the entire Disney organization that made Walt Disney's dream come true. May Walt Disney World bring Joy and Inspiration and New Knowledge to all who come to this happy place . . . a Magic Kingdom where the young at heart of all ages can laugh and play and learn - together."

During Walt Disney World's first year, over 10 million guests visited the park, and today, approximately 900 million guests from around the world have enjoyed its exciting attractions, thrilling stories and countless magical moments.

CHAPTER TWO

SECRETS OF THE MAGIC KINGDOM

"Here in Florida, we have something special we never enjoyed at Disneyland...the blessing of size. There's enough land here to hold all the ideas and plans we can possibly imagine."

- Walt Disney

Welcome!

We begin our tour of the hidden secrets and stories of Walt Disney World at the Magic Kingdom before continuing on to the rest of the parks.

As you make your way through the Magic Kingdom, you'll walk past, over and even through countless secrets and story elements just waiting to be discovered. Hidden Mickeys and cryptic messages hide in plain sight, while touching tributes and special guest experiences await only those who are "in the know." In the pages which follow, you'll discover the secrets of the Magic Kingdom to see and experience the park in an all new way! Let's begin at the entrance...

The Gang Says "Hello"

Sleep in and you'll miss this first secret. Each morning, Mickey Mouse, Minnie Mouse, Donald Duck, Goofy and the rest of the Disney character gang arrive aboard the grand Lilly Belle steam engine at the Main Street Railroad Station just prior to the opening of the Magic Kingdom to greet guests and welcome them to another day of wonder, magic and memories.

Only Chance of the Day

If you want to get a classic photo of the train engine, cars and Disney characters positioned directly in front of the Main Street Railroad Station, then the opening ceremony is the time to do it. Why? Because this is  the one and only time during the day in which the train engine is stopped directly in front of the station, complete with characters. All throughout the rest of the day the engine pulls forward and comes to a stop just past the station to allow guests to safely board the passenger cars.

Old to New Choo Choo

The oldest train engine is also the newest! From the Walt Disney Company...

"Built in 1916, almost a decade earlier than the Walter E. Disney and Roger E. Broggie train engines, the Roy O. Disney is the only steam engine that did not debut at the Magic Kingdom's opening on October 1, 1971. It was not until December of that year that it joined its three fellow passenger trains on the tracks at the Walt Disney World Railroad. The new train missed the Magic Kingdom's opening date by two months, and instead made the perfect Christmas gift for the new park: Roy O. Disney Number 4."

Tour the Railroad

Are you a big fan of the Walt Disney World Railroad? Want a behind the scenes look at what goes into maintaining the locomotives and preparing them for use each day at the Magic Kingdom? Then you're in luck! Disney offers the 3-hour "The Magic Behind Our Steam Trains" tour everyday, except Friday and Sunday.   Call 407-939-8687 to learn more and to make reservations.

CLICKS AND CLACKS AT THE TRACKS

After entering the park, stop and listen at the Main Street Railroad Station. Do you hear the telegraph working? That's the Morse Code rendition of a portion of Walt Disney's opening day speech at Disneyland on July 17, 1955, and it plays all throughout the day.

Note: Those guests who are skilled at understanding Morse Code may find the message tapped here to be unrecognizable. Why? Because the Imagineers, in their attention to detail, created it in the period specific "American Morse", also known as "Railroad Morse", which preceded today's "International Morse Code."

PAUSE FOR 100 YEARS

The Magic Kingdom awaits, but before you step into this magical world, take a moment to climb the stairs of the Main Street Railroad Station and step inside. It's easy to dismiss it as simply an old railroad station from the turn of the last century, but pause and consider the entire building was constructed in 1971!   Disney   Imagineers successfully captured the look, feel and essence of another era, one which ties seamlessly with turn-of-the-20th-century Main Street, U.S.A.

CRANK UP THE ACTION

Here's a secret which takes you back to another time for some old-fashioned fun, all for only a penny.

While in the Main Street Railroad Station, you'll find some antique cast iron "Clamshell" mutoscopes. Introduced in 1895, the mutoscope was one of the most popular machines in penny arcades across the country and provided customers with a form of moving entertainment before the era of motion pictures. Though they were wildly popular in their day,

mutoscopes such as these are extremely rare now. If you were to find one, chances are it wouldn't work, so this is truly a once-in-a-lifetime opportunity to see this unique form of turn-of-the-20th-century entertainment. Simply drop in a penny, peek into the viewer and turn the crank to watch an exciting, albeit brief, old movie.

Note: It's surprising to discover that the mutoscope, while patented by Herman Casler in 1894, was invented by none other than Winsor McCay, who played an important role in the life of Walt Disney. Inside each machine are over 800 cards, each of which is printed with a photographic image from approximately 50 feet of film, and these cards "flip" by rapidly as the user turns the crank. This is a process which is very similar to that of animated film, in which countless animated stills appear in rapid succession so as to give the illusion of fluid movement. It's only logical that Winsor McCay would go on to develop and publish in 1914 what is considered to be the very first cartoon featuring an animated character, titled *Gertie the Dinosaur*. This is the film which is recognized by The Walt Disney Company as having played an important role in inspiring a young 12 year-old Walt Disney to become an animator.

WHO KNOWS THE ROSE?

Now take a look at the floor of the train station. There in the middle is a large compass rose, which is only fitting for a train station from which guests disembark for distant lands. Stand in the middle of this compass rose and you will discover that Main Street, U.S.A. was built to perfectly align north and south.

A NOTE OF COINCIDENCE

Nearby, you'll find a beautifully restored orchestrion. Built in 1927 by the J.P. Seeburg Piano Company, its wooden cabinet is filled with numerous instruments, including a piano, a mandolin, a xylophone, castanets, a tambourine and more, all of which come to life to play old-fashioned music from the days of Steamboat Willie. Of note is that two employees of the J.P. Seeburg Company, Oscar Nelson and Peder Wiggen, struck out on their own in 1922 to start their own business. Observant guests will recognize an orchestrion similar to this model can be found inside the railroad station in Disneyland, and this was made by non other than the new Nelson-Wiggen Piano Company.

THE TICKET OFFICE

Step outside the train station and find the Ticket Office window out front. Peer inside and you'll find an interesting collection of vintage railroad items, including freight bills, oil cans, luggage tags and a genuine copy of Harper's Weekly from August 2, 1862. In addition, there on the wall are two old photos of historic steam engines. Study these closely, and you may find they look familiar.

The framed photo on the bottom is of the Magic Kingdom's Lilly Belle steam engine prior to her original refurbishment. Built in September of 1928 by Baldwin Locomotive Works, this grand engine was discovered by Roger Broggie and his team in the state of Yucatan in Mexico and refurbished in time for the Magic Kingdom's opening day on October 1, 1971.

Above the photo of the Lilly Belle is an image of an old steam engine sitting on rails at a sugar cane plantation in Louisiana. Though rusted and in a state of disrepair, this engine would be restored to become the bright and shiny Fred Gurley, which plys the tracks today at Disneyland in California.

A MAGICAL VIEW

Before you descend the stairs back to Town Square, take in the view of Main Street, U.S.A. from the balcony. This is perhaps one of the finest views of Cinderella Castle you'll find in the entire park and an excellent place from which to view Halloween, Christmas and other seasonal decorations.

A Subtle Trick of the Eye

You probably didn't notice as you approached the Magic Kingdom, but you were actually ascending a gradual slope as you walked. The ground you're standing on throughout the park is 14' higher than its original elevation. This is because Disney Imagineers needed to raise the "base" of the Magic Kingdom for two reasons; one was to hide the ten-foot high, twelve-foot wide corridors, or "Utilidors", which run beneath the park so as to allow for the unseen movement of supplies, materials and Cast Members during the day, and the other was to keep the park from flooding. The land upon which all of Walt Disney World Resort sits was semi-swampland when Walt bought it, so the Imagineers dug fill material from the bottom of a small lake in front of the Magic Kingdom and deposited it where you're now standing. This not only solved the swamp problem, but it also created the beautiful Seven Seas Lagoon you see today!

You're In The Movies

Unknown by many, Walt Disney designed the entrance to the Magic Kingdom to reveal itself as if you were walking into the opening of a Disney movie.

As you pass under the Main Street Railroad Station, you'll notice movie posters on the walls promoting the coming attractions in much the same way as movie trailers do in a theater. In this case, they promote the attractions you're about to experience during your day in the park. Next, the curtain "rises" as you emerge from the tunnels and take in the "opening act" of Town Square and Main Street, U.S.A. The story that is the Magic Kingdom begins to unfold as music fills the air, the scene reveals itself and the characters appear. Nearby is an old-fashioned popcorn cart. Always staged right by the entrance to Town Square, it offers fresh popped theater popcorn as a tasty treat. Next, as you begin to walk down Main Street, U.S.A., you'll see the "opening credits" displayed on the windows of

the second and third stories of the building facades. These "actors" are the names of the Disney Imagineers, Executives, Cast Members and others who played an important role in the creation of Walt Disney World and all the magic you're about to experience at the Magic Kingdom.

Fittingly, Walt Disney's name is the first and last one you'll see on Main Street, U.S.A., just as the Director of a movie is listed at both the opening and ending of the credits. Guests are greeted by a window at the Main Street Railroad Station which reads, "Walt Disney World Railroad Office - Keeping Dreams on Track - Walter E. Disney - Chief Engineer -". A second window for Walt Disney can be found at the far end of Main Street, U.S.A. on the second floor of the Plaza Ice Cream Parlor, facing Cinderella Castle.

Walt's brother, Roy O. Disney, was very instrumental in the creation of Walt Disney World and has a credit listed in a window above the Main Street Bakery. Having your name included on a Main Street, U. S. A.

window is considered one of the highest honors of working at The Walt Disney Company.

Chapter Three

Secrets of Town Square

"You can design and create and build the most wonderful place in the world, but it takes people to make the dream a reality.

- Walt Disney

A TRIBUTE TO WALT'S BROTHER

As you enter Town Square, take a moment to find the life-size bronze statue of Roy O. Disney and Minnie Mouse sitting on a park bench. It's a fitting tribute to Walt's brother, Roy O. Disney, and his tireless efforts to fulfill his brother's wishes to create Walt Disney World after Walt's passing in 1966.

Note: If you arrive shortly after the Magic Kingdom's opening, this area may be crowded with character greetings, so you may wish to visit it later in the day.

Nearby, you'll also find a bronze plaque which contains the text of Roy O. Disney's opening day remarks in 1971.

MAKE YOUR DAY SPECIAL

Happy Birthday!, Happy Anniversary! and Happy 1st Visit to the Magic Kingdom! If any one of these special occasions apply to your visit, or if you're newly married or on a family reunion, be sure to stop in at City Hall or one of the Vacation Planning Booths and ask for a button

which tells everyone of your special event. Cast Members will make a special effort to recognize you throughout your day at the park.

In Honor of Veterans

If you're a Veteran, then you're a special guest at the Magic Kingdom. Stop by Guest Relations in City Hall and inquire about participating in the daily Flag Retreat Ceremony in Town Square. Each evening, Disney officials escort a Veteran to the flagpole in the center of the square for an honorary lowering of the flag. The ceremony lasts about 15 minutes and is a patriotic event the entire family will enjoy. The ceremony typically begins at 5:00 p.m., though this time can vary with the time of year.

A Tribute to Opening Day

As you exit City Hall, notice the Fire Station next door, which houses Engine Company 71. More than just a random

number, the Disney Imagineers chose 71 in honor of the year in which the Magic Kingdom opened, 1971.

A Patchwork of Respect

Step inside the Fire Station and you'll discover a collection of antique fire-fighting equipment, as well as countless fire station patches and other insignias from stations all across the country honoring the brave men and women who serve and protect us on a daily basis.

A Personal Character Visit

Not all Disney characters appear according to the schedule published in the Daily Times Guide. Sometimes they will emerge quietly from an out-of-the-way doorway to welcome guests, have their picture taken and sign autographs. The back of the Fire Station is one such location, so take a moment to stop in and see if, by chance, you can have a rare solitary visit with a favorite Disney character.

Look Good For Your Visit

Now journey next door to find the old-fashioned Harmony Barber Shop, established in 1886. The secret . . . it's a real barber shop, and you can actually get your hair cut in the Magic Kingdom! Skilled barbers will trim, style, color and coif your hair, topping it all off with colorful pixie dust to give you a styling or even festive look for a day in the park. A "My First Haircut" package, which is popular with young children, provides patrons with their very first hair cut, special Mickey Mouse ears and a certificate honoring the occasion. And if you're lucky, you may even be serenaded by the Dapper Dans barbershop quartet.

Although small and quaint, the Harmony Barber Shop performs between 350 and 400 services a week. Children's "First Haircuts" are the establishment's specialty. If you arrive at the park's opening, or shortly thereafter, plan on waiting in line.

GAWRSH, THAT'S FUNNY!

Now stroll across the Town Square and find Goofy sitting on a bench in front of Tony's Town Square Restaurant. While others pass by or stop only briefly to get a picture, go ahead and sit down next to him. You may be surprised to find he thinks it's funny.

Note: Sometimes Goofy can be found elsewhere in the Town Square, as he likes to move around.

TONY'S TOWN SQUARE RESTAURANT

Tony's Town Square Restaurant? It's named for the Italian Chef who served the romantic spaghetti dinner to the two title characters, Lady and Tramp, in the 1955 classic Disney animated film "Lady and the Tramp."

LADY AND THE TRAMP IMPRINTS

Many Magic Kingdom secrets are hidden right out in the open, where they are walked over by countless guests without their ever noticing. The brown area in the streets of Liberty Square, the Bride's wedding ring at the Haunted Mansion, even the Utilidors. Here is another one you will not notice unless you look down. Make your way to the base of the stairs leading up to the dining area at Tony's Town Square Restaurant and you'll find a large heart with paw prints belonging to Lady and the Tramp imprinted into the sidewalk.

CALL WAITING

Now take a moment to step into The Chapeau, where you'll find an antique phone mounted on the wall. Most guests assume it's just a prop and walk right past it, but those who look closer find otherwise. Pick it up and listen in on a fun conversation between a mother and her daughter, Annie. Being the turn of the 20th century, Annie's mother is surprised that ham has now reached 11 cents per pound, and with things now so expensive, she advises Annie to marry a man who has $300 in savings and earns at least $8 per week.

Note: The phone above, which is a photo of the actual phone inside The Chapeau, courtesy of Dave Drumheller of

WDWGuidedTours.com, is a second generation Western Electric Picture Frame Front Model 317 Wall Telephone.

HAPPY BIRTHDAY TO YOU!

If it's your birthday, then don't pass by this opportunity to make it really special. While in The Chapeau, find a "Mickey Mouse Ears Happy Birthday Hat". Much more than the celebratory birthday button you can pick up for free at City Hall, it announces your special day with a colorful and festive hat that lets everyone know you're another year "funner".

Note: Other festive birthday hats are also available by calling Merchandise Guest Services at 877-560-6477 or visit www.DisneyParks.com/store.

NO GUMMING UP THE WORKS

As you journey throughout the Magic Kingdom today, notice you won't find bits of gum all over the sidewalk, under benches, stuck to railings, or elsewhere. That's because, as with Disneyland, gum isn't sold anywhere in Walt Disney World Resort.

27 STEPS TO A CLEANER PARK

This next secret is a display of behavioral science. As you enter Main Street, U.S.A., notice that the trash cans are no more than 27 paces apart. When building Disneyland Resort, Walt Disney visited other amusement parks at the time and studied just how far their visitors would go to drop trash in a trashcan. He found that any distance greater than 27 paces would lead people to just drop their trash on the ground. Today, trashcans are placed at convenient distances of no more than 27 paces throughout Walt Disney World Resort to keep the parks clean and provide a higher quality guest experience.

CHAPTER FOUR

SECRETS OF
MAIN STREET, U.S.A.

"Main Street, U.S.A. is America at the turn of the century – the crossroads of an era. The gas lamps and the electric lamp – the horse drawn car and auto car. Main Street is everyone's hometown – the heart line of America."

- Walt Disney

FORCED PERSPECTIVE

As you begin to "walk right down the middle of Main Street, U.S.A.", study the architecture for a classic Disney trick of the eye. Here the Imagineers designed and built the buildings on Main Street, U.S.A. with an optical illusion called "Forced Perspective." Using this technique, they made the buildings appear taller than they actually are. The street level floors were built to full scale at 12 feet in height, while the second story was built slightly smaller at 10 feet and the third story smaller still at 8 feet. In addition, the windows of the second and third stories were built both narrower and shorter than the windows below to further the illusion of height.

THE DAWN OF A NEW ERA

As with Main Street, U.S.A. in Disneyland, the Magic Kingdom's Main Street, U.S.A. represents many things, one of which is the dawn of a new era and an exciting moment in history...the arrival of new technologies and the advent of electricity. Gas lamps are being replaced with electric street lamps, horse-drawn trolleys share the road with motorized jitneys and the facade of the buildings are beginning to be adorned with bright new electric bulbs.

Perhaps one of the best examples Disney Imagineers used in capturing this transition to electricity and the new age is reflected in the street lamps adorning Main Street, U.S.A. If you stop and look, you'll notice they all have a gas flame. There was a time in America's history in which all street lamps were powered by gas, and each evening Lamplighters would make their way from lamp to lamp to light the flames as darkness approached. As you make your way to the end of Main Street, U.S.A. and into the plaza area in front of Cinderella Castle, take note of how the lamps have changed. Instead of a single gas flame, each lamppost now uses the latest technology... multiple incandescent light bulbs powered by the "new" electricity of the era.

AMERICA'S FIRST STREET LAMP

On February 7, 1817, Baltimore, Maryland made history with the installation of the very first gas street lamp used in the United States. Standing at the corner of North Holliday and East Baltimore streets, it dutifully performed its task for 180 years before being replaced with a replica in 1997. Today, as the only working gas street lamp remaining in Baltimore, this single lamp stands on that corner as a monument to its important role in American history.

When designing Main Street, U.S.A., the Imagineers could have chosen any one of the hundreds of gas street lamp designs which were in use across the country during the turn of the 20th century. However, they instead chose a design with historical significance. The gas street lamps guests see lining Main Street, U.S.A. are *exact duplicates* of the historical lamp found in Baltimore, and as such each represents the very first gas street lamp used in America.

Note: When Baltimore began selling its surplus gas lamps in the 1950s, a number of them were bought by Imagineer Emile Kuri for installation at Disneyland, where they are in use today. While these are similar in design, they are not exact duplicates of the first gas lamp used in the United States, nor those installed on Walt Disney World's Main Street, U.S.A. in the Magic Kingdom.

HORSE AND BUGGY AND JITNEY

Main Street, U.S.A. represents an exciting time of change in turn-of-the-20th-century America, and another accurate representation of this are the colorful Main Street Vehicles transporting guests up and down the street.

In 1900, all modes of transportation on America's streets, including trolleys, buggies and carts, were pulled by horses, but beginning in 1905, the automobile began to make its appearance, and by 1915 horse pulled vehicles were largely a thing of the past. On Main Street, U.S.A., guests are immersed in this same transitional period in history as they are surrounded by both horse drawn and combustion powered vehicles transporting guests on their way to magic and adventure.

ALONE ON MAIN STREET, U.S.A.

Do you wish you could have Main Street, U.S.A. all to yourself? Without all the crowds and with an unobstructed view of Cindrella Castle, perfect for taking pictures? With this next secret, you just might.

Disney offers an informative tour called Marceline to Magic Kingdom, which begins at 8:15 a.m. Book this tour on a morning in which The Magic Kingdom opens at 9:00 a.m. *and you'll be allowed into the park 45 minutes early. Arrive even earlier, and you may have time available to stroll up and down Main Street, U.S.A. while the tour assembles.* Be sure to have your camera ready, because this is the moment you've been waiting for! As one who has had the pleasure of photographing Main Street, U.S.A. before it has opened to guests, I can tell you that this is a surreal, yet very amazing experience.

You can book this tour by calling 407-939-8687. As an alternative, you may also book an early breakfast at Cinderella's Royal Table. This will also get you into The Magic Kingdom early, but you will not be able to move about, and it is much more expensive than the Marceline to Magic Kingdom tour.

Walt's Boyhood Town

As with Disneyland, the Magic Kingdom's Main Street, U.S.A. is modeled after the town Walt Disney lived in as a young boy, Marceline, Missouri.

A Window into History

You'll often hear that Walt designed the storefront windows of Main Street, U.S.A. to be low so that even small children could easily look inside and see their magical displays, but this is actually a "Magic Kingdom urban legend." Instead, the low window displays are another example of the Imagineers' attention to detail.

As indicated by the "Est. 1886" sign on the Harmony Barber Shop in Town Square, Main Street, U.S.A. represents turn-of-the-20th-century America. In this era, before the Internet, television and even radio, shop owners had to rely upon their window displays as their primary means of advertising. As a result, they typically built them as large as they could, often reaching nearly to the sidewalk, so as to show off as much merchandise as possible to passing customers.

Sounds Like Disney Whimsy

Here's a fun secret which Disney Imagineers created to capture the small town feel of Main Street, U.S.A. while adding another hidden story element with a whimsical touch. Like so many secrets, it's revealed only to those who pause and observe. As you journey up Main Street, U.S.A., take a right on

Center Street and look for the windows at the end of the street which read, "Singing Lessons" and "Music and Dance Lessons." Listen carefully below the windows and you'll eavesdrop on some rather comical encounters!

A Fun New Perspective

It's so easy to dismiss the vehicles of Main Street, U.S.A. as only simple attractions which pale in comparison to some of the classics, such as Pirates of the Caribbean or Space Mountain, but they are actually a key to a whole new way to experience the magic.

If it's your very first visit to the Magic Kingdom, then you'll want to "stroll right down the middle of Main Street, U.S.A.", but if you've been many times, then do not walk past these attractions, but instead make it a point to hop aboard the Horse and Trolley, a Main Street Jitney or Fire Engine #71 while in Town Square and *ride down Main Street, U.S.A.* while enjoying the tremendous view as it unfolds all around you. It's an exciting new way to experience this portion of the park as you ride through the hustle and bustle towards Cinderella Castle.

Legendary Guest Service

Disney's commitment to the guest experience is legendary. As you visit the shops on Main Street, U.S.A., be aware that should you purchase anything and it breaks during your visit, Disney will replace it free of charge. This includes broken souvenirs, lost balloons, even dropped trays of food, ice cream, churros, etc.

Tip: Here's a tip just for parents. If your child really

wants a Mickey or Minnie Mouse balloon to make their day at the Magic Kingdom extra special, you'll discover they're sometimes hard to find. Head over to Main Street, U.S.A. and there's a good chance you'll find a balloon vendor near Center Street, especially early in the day.

ONE OF WALT'S FAVORITE TREATS

As you make your way down Main Street, U.S.A., you are surrounded by tributes to Cast Members, notable Imagineers and even Walt Disney himself.

At the far end of Main Street, U.S.A. sits the Plaza Ice Cream Parlor, where guests will find two tributes to Walt. The first is the parlor itself. Ice cream was one of Walt's favorite treats, so he made sure to include the Gibson Girl Ice Cream Parlor in Disneyland so his guests could also enjoy this tasty treat. Here, in the Magic Kingdom, the Imagineers have paid tribute to Walt and his vision by including the Plaza Ice Cream Parlor when they designed the park. The second tribute is a large window dedicated to "Walter E. Disney", which you will find on the balcony of the Plaza Ice Cream Parlor, behind a railing. Fittingly, it faces Cinderella Castle.

THE SMOKE TREE RANCH

Now make your way to the "Partners" statue of Walt and Mickey Mouse and closely study Walt's tie. There you will find a symbol made up of three letters, "STR", which refer to the Smoke Tree Ranch in Palm Springs, California. Walt and his wife, Lillian, greatly enjoyed visiting the ranch whenever Walt could take a break from his many different projects. In fact, they enjoyed it so much that they chose to build a second home there. However, Walt sold the home to help fund the

construction of Disneyland, but this turned out to be a wise decision, as Disneyland proved to be such a success that he later built a new home at Smoke Tree Ranch, one which was even larger than the original.

WATCHING "WISHES" FROM CALIFORNIA

At the end of the day, many guests choose to watch "Wishes", the fireworks spectacular, from Main Street, U.S.A. This is a great spot to see one of the best shows in the park, as the fireworks appear directly over Cinderella Castle. However, unknown to many, you can also see the fireworks from The California Grill, found at the top of the Contemporary Resort just outside the park. At the time of the show, the restaurant dims the lights and plays the same music heard at the Magic Kingdom. It's a unique perspective on this magical attraction.

Tip: Guests will also find many other locations throughout the Magic Kingdom offer a fun new perspective on Wishes, including Fantasyland, Splash Mountain and even Disney's Polynesian Resort.

CHAPTER FIVE

SECRETS OF ADVENTURELAND

"Here is adventure. Here is romance. Here is mystery. Tropical rivers – silently flowing into the unknown. The unbelievable splendor of exotic flowers...the eerie sound of the jungle...with eyes that are watching. This is Adventureland."

- Walt Disney

BWANA BOB

You may have noticed on your way into Adventureland a merchandise kiosk called Bwana Bob's. Adorned with a thatched roof, tribal masks and bamboo, this kiosk offering hats, sunglasses, souvenirs and more is an homage to Bob Hope, who, as a fan of Walt Disney and his work, was the star of the 1963 film, *Call Me Bwana*, and a guest on the NBC TV special which opened Walt Disney World in October of 1971.

A TRIBUTE TO MARC DAVIS

Hidden throughout Walt Disney World and Disneyland Resort are tributes to many Cast Members and Disney Imagineers who played a very important role in not only developing the theme parks, but The Walt Disney Company, as well. Many of these tributes are hidden in different attractions. For example, in the treasure room of the Pirates of the Caribbean, Disney Imagineers have placed a coat of arms with the name "Marco Daviso." It is a tribute to Marc Davis, one of Disney's "Nine Old Men" and the man responsible for animating many of Disney's well known characters, including Tinker Bell, Cruella De Vil and Cinderella, among others. In addition, he was responsible for the story and character development of many classic Disney attractions, including the Haunted Mansion, "it's a small world", The Jungle Cruise and, of course, Pirates of the Caribbean.

CHECK THE CHECKMATE, MATE

As you enter the Pirates of the Caribbean attraction, take the right queue line instead of the left and stop to peer into the dungeon windows on the right, shortly after you pass the turnstiles. There you will discover two chess-playing skeletons below. The rumor is their match is deadlocked in a tie, which makes for a great story, but if you're a student of the game, you may think otherwise.

Note: Periodically, the pawns on the board are moved.

PLEASE WATCH YOUR STEP ...AND YOUR PEG!

You may have noticed as you exit many attractions throughout the park and step upon a moving walkway that footprints are painted on the walkway surface to indicate the direction in which guests should proceed. Take note of the "foot prints" the Imagineers have placed on the moving walkway as you exit the Pirates of the Caribbean attraction. Those are the markings belonging to a peg-legged pirate!

DOLE WHIP

Turkey legs, Mickey Mouse ice cream bars and even churros are some of the iconic treats at Walt Disney World, yet the popular Dole Whip holds a special place in many guests' hearts, and a trip to the Magic Kingdom wouldn't be complete without one. In fact, the Dole Whip is such a treasured tradition it even has its own collectible pin!

Admittedly, this is a well-known "secret", but if you're like the many who have walked right past the Dole Whip counter while wondering why there is a long line, then you need to stop and find out why. They're lining up for the delicious Dole Whip, a classic Magic Kingdom treat you'll remember long after your vacation ends. Look for the Dole Whip next to the Enchanted Tiki-Room, opposite The Magic Carpets of Aladdin.

Tip: You can also get a Dole Whip at the Pineapple Lanai at Disney's Polynesian Resort.

NOW A ROUGH ADVENTURE

Now pause for a moment and notice one of the subtle changes which has occurred since you left Main Street, U.S.A. No longer are there streets defined by level brick walkways and crisp curbs, but instead you find rough uneven paths disappearing into the undergrowth, and instead of the finely pruned trees and shrubs of the Hub, the jungle is overgrown...perfect for an adventure.

THE MAGIC CARPETS OF ALADDIN

One of the fun secrets about the Magic Kingdom is how Disney Imagineers often whimsically extend the story of an attraction beyond the attraction itself, and The Magic Carpets of Aladdin is a perfect example of this.

As you approach the attraction, find the large golden camel near the attraction's sign. Camels, such as those in Aladdin's world, are known to spit, and this one is no exception. Here the Imagineers have arranged for this camel to periodically "spit" water at passing guests, often with surprising accuracy!

A CHARMING HIDDEN MICKEY

Upon leaving The Magic Carpets of Aladdin, make your way to the entrance of the Agrabah Bazaar to find a small Hidden Mickey which thousands of guests walk over each and every day without ever realizing it is there.

Near the entrance to the Agrabah Bazaar is a pole holding up a fabric awning. Not far from the base of the pole is a group of white stones set into the pavement, and not far from these stones is a metal charm which holds a Hidden Mickey, no doubt dropped by a peddler selling his wares. Photo courtesy of WDWGuidedTours.com

CHAPTER SIX

SECRETS OF FRONTIERLAND

"Here we experience the story of our country's past...the colorful drama of Frontier America in the exciting days of the covered wagon and the stagecoach...the advent of the railroad...and the romantic riverboat. Frontierland is a tribute to the faith, courage, and ingenuity of the pioneers who blazed the trails across America."

- Walt Disney

Addressing This Secret

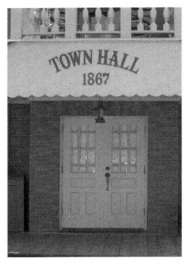

The stage that is the Magic Kingdom is filled with countless small details, most of which are easily overlooked, yet when discovered reveal another interesting element of the story. For example, take a look at the address numbers found throughout Frontierland.

Note how they are not in chronological order, but instead are designed to represent the year in which the building was constructed. The Hall of Presidents was built in 1787, while the Town Hall of Frontierland was built in 1867 and the General Store in 1876.

A.C. Dietz Company Lanterns

If you mosey over to the General Store in Frontierland, you'll see on an exterior wall a small sign next to an oil lamp which reads, "A.C. Dietz Co. - Importer of Coal Oil Lamps - Hardware - Harness - A Complete Line of Saddles."

Typically, in a manner similar to the windows on Main Street, U.S.A., a sign such as this pays homage to an individual who played an important role within The Walt Disney Company, such as a notable animator, an innovative Imagineer, or someone who helped build Walt Disney World Resort. However, in this case, this sign recognizes someone outside the world of Disney with an obscure but definite connection to Walt Disney and the early days of Disneyland!

In 1955, when Walt was building his brand new park, Disneyland, he bought all of the lanterns used in Frontierland from the R.E. Dietz Lantern Company. That appears to be a clear connection to this sign, but nobody named A.C. Dietz had ever worked for the company. However, the Founder, Robert E. Dietz, did have a cousin in San Francisco who owned and ran a General Store during the 1850s much like the one upon which this sign is affixed. Located at 224 Front Street, it provided all of the supplies the rugged forty-niners of the California Gold Rush needed to work their claims, including harnesses and saddles for their horses, bags of grain, wire, mining equipment and coal oil lanterns made by the Dietz Lantern Company. And the name of this cousin who owned the General Store... *Alfred Clinch Dietz*!

Now if you were to look closely at the lantern hanging on the wall next to the A.C. Dietz sign, you would assume it was made by the Dietz Lantern Company, but instead it was manufactured by W.T. Kirkman Lanterns, Inc. Why isn't it a Dietz Lantern? Because the original Dietz lanterns Walt bought for Disneyland and the early days of Walt Disney World were manufactured using components made of tin. Unfortunately, those components wore out over time and the lanterns needed replacing. The Disney Imagineers turned to W.T. Kirkman Lanterns to provide them with new galvanized steel models, which do not rust, but instead stand up better in today's weather...or that of the 1850s. (Or in this case, 1876, which ties in with the address of the Frontierland General Store.)

My thanks to Woody Kirkman of W.T. Kirkman Lanterns, Inc. for his generous contribution to this story. Photo courtesy of WDWGuidedTours.com

UNCLE KEPPLE & SONS

Visit the General Store in Frontierland, and you're likely to see some bags of "Uncle Kepple & Sons" livestock feed. On the face of it, this is a simple nod to Walt Disney's grandfather, Kepple Disney. However, as with many of the Disney Imagineers' secrets, there's a bit more to this intriguing story.

Based upon the nearby sign referring to A.C. Dietz, who ran a General Store like the one in Frontierland in San Francisco during the California Gold Rush, one could assume these bags acknowledge Kepple Disney's setting out in 1877 with his sons Robert and Elias (Walt's father) on a journey to California to search for gold. They never made it, however, as Kepple instead decided to stop and settle in Kansas, where he purchased over 300 acres in Ellis County from the Union Pacific Railroad and established a farm. Photo courtesy of WDWGuidedTours.com

FRONTIERLAND SHOOTIN' ARCADE

They don't know it, but many guests walk past The Frontierland Shootin' Arcade and miss out on an opportunity to practice their shooting technique for free. Be one of the first guests of the day to stop by  and test your shooting prowess and you may be rewarded with a few free rounds, as each morning random rifles at the Frontierland Shootin' Arcade are "pre-loaded" with rounds on the house.

Note: The Frontierland Shootin' Arcade is a classic attraction which dates back to opening day at Disneyland, and it is one of the few attractions in the park which requires an extra fee.

A HIDDEN MICKEY SET IN STONE

Thousands and thousands of guests walk by everyday without ever noticing it, but hidden from view on the bridge to the lower section of Splash Mountain is a classic Hidden Mickey made of three stones.  To find it, look on the bridge support which faces towards Tom Sawyer Island.

HARPER'S MILL

Harper's Mill on Tom Sawyer Island is another attraction element which pays tribute to a notable Disney Cast Member. Disney Legend Harper Goff was a Disney Imagineer, artist and production designer involved in the design and production of notable Disney films, as well as Main Street, U.S.A., the Jungle Cruise at Disneyland and World Showcase at Epcot.

It is rumored that the creaks and groans of the mill wheel of Harper's Mill on Tom Sawyer Island actually play "Down by the Old Mill Stream". However, I've listened and didn't find this to be the case. Others swear by it, though. That said, make sure you find your way onto Tom Sawyer Island and peer inside Harper's Mill to see the large spinning gears. It's an attention to detail many guests miss and really adds to the Tom Sawyer Island story

TOM PICKED UP
ALL THE BRUSHES

Here's a classic Walt Disney World Secret that is no more. It used to be that a special prize awaited those guests who found this next secret...a FastPass to Splash Mountain or Big Thunder Mountain Railroad.

At the beginning of each day, cast members would hide a few paint brushes throughout Tom Sawyer Island. Each would be covered in whitewash and read...

"Tom Sawyer Paintbrush - In order to complete his chores, Tom needs to whitewash Aunt Polly's fence. Unfortunately, in his play time, he managed to lose the brushes all over the island. If you happen to pick up this brush, please return it to the raft driver. Remember only one brush per family. Thank you."

Lucky guests who found a paintbrush could return it to the raft driver and receive a FastPass for Splash Mountain or Big Thunder Mountain, which was valid all day long. However, both Tom and Huck returned to Hannibal a while ago and picked up all the brushes, so they are no longer hidden for guests to find. Perhaps one day Tom will lose them again.

A LITERARY FENCE

Give it a casual glance and you'll think it's just a work in progress. An unpainted fence waiting for someone to come along and finish the job, but if you look again and pay attention to the names and the

color, you'll see it's the famed whitewashed fence from the classic Mark Twain tale, "The Adventures of Tom Sawyer."

Pappy's Pier

Head over to the other side of Tom Sawyer Island, opposite Big Thunder Mountain Railroad, and you'll find Pappy's Pier, a quiet out-of-the-way dock with a couple of wooden rocking chairs and an entertaining view of Big Thunder Mountain Railroad and the passing Liberty Belle riverboat.

Big Thunder Mountain Railroad

Ask someone in the know, and they will tell you that where you sit on some attraction vehicles makes all the difference in the world. Want to make your ride on Big Thunder Mountain even more exciting? Then enter  the queue line and ask a Cast Member if you may sit in the back car of the attraction where the "wildest ride in the wilderness" is even wilder.

A Different Tune at Night

Pass by the town of Tumbleweed at Big Thunder Mountain Railroad during the day and you'll notice that things are awfully quiet, as the miners are out working in the mines, but at night the town comes alive with lights, noise and music.

LYTUM & HYDE
EXPLOSIVES COMPANY

The Imagineers' attention to detail in the queue lines is legendary, and Big Thunder Mountain is no exception. As you make your way along, pay attention to the authentic antique mining gear inside and out, all of which was discovered by Disney Imagineers in the West and brought in specifically for this attraction. In addition, take note of the (open!) cases of dynamite stacked next to the mine entrance as you careen through the attraction. In another nod to the Imagineers' sense of humor, these cases read "Lytum & Hyde Explosives Company", and the wording on the side of the casket "sign" above for the Tumbleweed Cabinet & Casket Co., reads "Furniture, Upholstery, & Embalming." Truly the wild west, indeed! Photo courtesy of WDWGuidedTours.com

THE FUSING CAGE

As you make your way through the queue of Big Thunder Mountain Railroad, you'll notice the door to the "Fusing Cage" is adorned with the names of notable Disney Imagineers who contributed to the development of the attraction. Here's a short bio for each...

Little Big Gibson - Blaine Gibson

In addition to providing animation for early Disney classic films, including Fantasia, Peter Pan and Sleeping Beauty, Blaine Gibson created hundreds of accurately detailed sculptures for such attractions as Great Moments with Mr. Lincoln, the Haunted Mansion, Pirates of the Caribbean and more. Perhaps his most famous work is of the bronze statue "Partners", which depicts Walt and Mickey standing hand in hand and can be found in the hub of Disney theme parks around the world.

Jolley the Kid - Bob Jolley

As Field Art Director, Bob Jolley used his Imagineering talents to combine Big Thunder Mountain Railroad's shiny new technology with its authentic mining past. Recognized as an expert in show finishes and skilled in the craft of aging story elements, he blended the new and old together to give the entire attraction the rustic historic look we see today.

Buckaroo Burke - Pat Burke

Pat Burke was the WDI Imagineer responsible for designing many of the attractions found throughout Disney theme parks worldwide, including four Big Thunder Mountains, four Indiana Jones, three Jungle Cruises and the original Splash Mountain. It is commonly known among guests that the authentic mining equipment found throughout the different Big Thunder Mountain attractions came from many different locations across the United States, and Pat Burke was the man who was responsible for discovering it all and bringing it to the parks.

Calamity Clem - Clem Hall

Clem Hall was a concept artist responsible for creating conceptual artwork for numerous Disneyland and Walt Disney World attractions, including Big Thunder Mountain Railroad.

Skittish Skip - Skip Lange

Skip Lange of Walt Disney Imagineering was responsible for designing the unique mountain landscape of Disneyland's Big Thunder Mountain Railroad, fashioning the look after the "hoodoos" found in Bryce Canyon National Park in Utah. He would go on to design the rockwork for every Big Thunder Mountain Railroad attraction found in Disney theme parks worldwide.

Wild Wolf Joerger - Fred Joerger

An important part of every attraction's development is the crafting of miniature 3-D models which represent how the attraction will look when finished. Fred Joerger, in addition to crafting models for early Disney movie sets and "most everything at Disneyland", was known as the "resident rock expert" because of his expertise in designing and crafting the large realistic stonework found throughout Disneyland and Walt Disney World, including the stonework found at the Jungle Cruise, Pirates of the Caribbean and Big Thunder Mountain Railroad.

Matchstick Marc – Marc Davis

This is a tribute to a Disney Legend and one of Disney's "Nine Old Men" of animation, Marc Davis. In addition to animating such classic Disney characters as Cinderella, Snow White, Tinker Bell, Cruella De Vil, Brer Rabbit, Bambi, Alice and others, Mr. Davis played an important role in the development of characters for many of your favorite attractions, including Pirates of the Caribbean, The Jungle Cruise, "it's a small world", The Country Bear Jamboree, the Haunted Mansion, The Enchanted Tiki Room and more.
This isn't the only homage to Marc Davis in the park, as guests will also find a tombstone at the Haunted Mansion which reads...

In Memory Of
Our Patriarch
Dear Departed
Grandpa
Marc

Mama Hutchinson – Helena Hutchinson

Helena Hutchinson practiced her craft in the Figure Finishing department at Walt Disney Imagineering, which was responsible for adorning the multitude of characters that appeared in the parks, be they birds, goats, buffaloes, tigers, skeletons or human figures, in everything from fur and paint to feathers and costumes. As an expert in working with fur, she finished the animals found throughout Big Thunder Mountain Railroad.

A TRIBUTE TO TONY WAYNE BAXTER

Hidden throughout Big Thunder Mountain Railroad at the Magic Kingdom, and every park where this attraction exists, is a clever tribute to the Disney Imagineer credited with its creation. Located on the Builders Plates of each locomotive, as well as on signs and old equipment, is a logo which includes the initials "BTM". On first glance, this is clearly a reference to "Big Thunder Mountain". However, if you study the "M", you'll see it looks more like an inverted "W", which it is. Pat Burke, the Disney Imagineer who acquired all of the antique mining equipment you see all around you from throughout the west, as well as gave the attraction its "rusty" look, purposely created this logo with the "W" upside down, so as to provide a cleverly hidden homage to the attraction's creator, Tony Wayne Baxter.

PROFESSOR CUMULUS ISOBAR

It passes by so quickly it's difficult to see, but just before you roar past the flooded town of Tumbleweed and dive into the Dave V. Jones Mine, look left and notice the wagon of Professor Cumulus Isobar, Rain Maker. Look quickly and you'll find the professor himself leaning out the front door while bailing out his wagon, all while his two donkeys stand to the side high and dry. His name, of course, is a nod to the Disney Imagineers' sometimes whimsical nature, as "Cumulus" is a type of cloud and "Isobar" is a measure of barometric pressure.

Tip: The scene of Professor Cumulus Isobar flies right by as you're riding Big Thunder Mountain Railroad, but if you'd like to see a slower perspective of Big Thunder Mountain and get a shot similar to the one above, then hop aboard the Walt Disney World Railroad at the Main Street or Frontierland Stations and have your camera ready as the train travels past the scene.

A Unique
Big Thunder Mountain Photo

All throughout the Magic Kingdom there are countless different perspectives of the park which everyone enjoys...the view of Cinderella Castle from Main Street, U.S.A., Splash Mountain from below the log flume drop, the pillaging pirates within Pirates of the Caribbean and perhaps a million others visible everywhere guests turn, and while these perspectives of the story that is the Magic Kingdom are certainly a thrill, the real fun is discovering the rare new perspectives of the park which few guests ever see...Frontierland from *inside* the Liberty Square Riverboat wheelhouse, the town of Tumbleweed from the Walt Disney World Railroad or perhaps even Main Street, U.S.A. from within the horse-pulled trolley.

Here's a new perspective of a favorite attraction which the Disney Imagineers have purposely hidden for you to find, yet

99% of guests miss. Even better, it gives you an opportunity to capture a dramatic photo of Big Thunder Mountain unlike any other!

As you approach Big Thunder Mountain Railroad, walk up and to the right towards the exit area. There you will find two exits to the attraction. Make your way to the top level exit and turn left at the fence where guests stop to watch the mine trains. Just before reaching the doorway, look for a large "crack" in the rocks on your right-hand side. If you stop here and look through the crack, you'll notice you can see the tracks from this hidden dead-on perspective.  Now zoom in with your camera and take a picture just as the next train engine exits the mine and you'll have a fun photo unlike any other which gives the impression you were standing right on the tracks as the train raced towards you! Photos courtesy of WDWGuidedTours.com

Splash Mountain

An FSU Weasel?

As you make your way through Splash Mountain, you'll begin to round a bend and spot Brer Fox holding Brer Rabbit inside a bee hive. Before reaching the bend, look up and spot a critter in the ceiling known by many as the "FSU Weasel," which periodically emerges and shouts something. Some believe it says, "FSU!", while others believe it's "If I's you!", a nod to the storyline which tells you at this point in the ride "I'd be turnin' around, if I was you.", for it is here you begin your climb to the 52 foot plunge into the briar patch!

All 'Board!...
The Zip-A-Dee Lady

This next secret is discovered only by those who make the effort to ride the Grand Circle Tour of the Walt Disney World Railroad, and of those who do see the secret, it usually takes them by surprise. Board the Walt Disney World Railroad and keep watch to the right hand side as the train passes into Splash Mountain. Here, guests aboard the train are treated to a fun overhead perspective of other guests riding logs through

Splash Mountain below as they make their way through the musical scene with the "Zip-A-Dee Lady" paddlewheeler.

ZIP-A-DEE HIDDEN MICKEY

The "Zip-A-Dee Lady" paddlewheeler scene also holds another classic Hidden Mickey, which, though easy to see, is a bit difficult to decipher. As you make your way through the scene in the hollowed-out Splash Mountain log,

look up and to the right of the paddlewheeler to find a large cloud. Study it carefully, and you'll find it's actually an image of Mickey Mouse lying on his back.

A HIDDEN REST

Parents wishing to give children a break can find the Laughin' Place play area in the shade under the train trestle by Splash Mountain. It can also be a great place for children to play while parents enjoy a ride or rest for a while.

Railroad Morse

As you make your way through the queue to board the Walt Disney World Railroad, notice the door to the left at the top of the ramp. As with the New Orleans Train Station at Disneyland and the Main Street Railroad Station at the Magic Kingdom, the "Railroad Morse" code being tapped out from behind this door is a portion of Walt Disney's opening day speech at Disneyland in 1955.

CHAPTER SEVEN

SECRETS OF
LIBERTY SQUARE

"Our heritage and ideals, our code and standards – the things we live by and teach our children – are preserved or diminished by how freely we exchange ideas and feelings."

- Walt Disney

THE HAUNTED MANSION

As you approach the Haunted Mansion, you'll notice a horseless funeral carriage out front. It's horseless in that the horse is there...but it isn't. Disney Imagineers continue the story of the Haunted Mansion well beyond the mansion itself with this creative story element mixed with the use of "themed paving". Look down and you will notice the horse's hoof prints are imprinted in the pavement and stretch from the carriage house out front to its final resting place beyond.

BEWARE OF BAD LUCK

Ninety-nine percent of guests miss this next secret, but you'll be lucky enough to see it...or will you?

Up near the rafters in the carriage house out front, you'll notice a number of horseshoes hanging from pegs. Horseshoes are to be hung with the ends facing up, so as to catch and hold good luck. Unfortunately, all of these horseshoes are hung with the ends facing down, signifying all the good luck has run out...just as you are about to enter the Haunted Mansion.

Nightly Apparitions

From the horseless carriage to the pet cemetery, the Haunted Mansion experience begins well before guests enter the front door.

Those who visit the attraction at night will notice a story element which is missing during the day. Stop in the queue line across from the front door of the mansion and find the window above the door. Pause long enough and you will notice it is often frequented by a couple of ghosts who can be seen walking by the window with a lantern in hand.

A Doomed Lawn

This next secret is one which requires guests to again pause and take notice, as most simply walk past and overlook it. It's a bit of a light-hearted secret, but a key element in telling the story of the Haunted  Mansion. Pause for a moment in the queue line and look at the lawn. Notice anything different here? Disney horticulturists are some of the finest in the world, and they go to great lengths to ensure the landscaping all throughout Walt Disney World Resort is impeccable, be it at the Magic Kingdom or your hotel. Topiaries are shaped into whimsical Disney characters, flowers are blooming at every turn and every plant you see is green, lush and well tended. However, here the horticulturists have purposely neglected the lawn of The Haunted Mansion so it remains brown...and dead.

A Persistent Ring

Here's a Haunted Mansion secret which was buried...but wouldn't die.

Years ago, a turnstile at the exit of The Haunted Mansion was removed by Disney Imagineers. Part of this turnstile involved a support pipe about the diameter of a finger, and when this pipe was cut flush at its base, it left a "ring" in the pavement, a ring which soon took on a life of its own. Guests noticing the "ring" surmised that this was a wedding ring which belonged to the Bride. No doubt it was crushed here in a moment of rage, jealousy or perhaps even murder! Since this was not part of the official Haunted Mansion story, but instead only a tale which endured as legend and myth, Disney eventually paved over this piece of pipe when reimagining the queue line. However, with the disappearance of the Bride's ring, Disney guests became as enraged as Master Gracey, and a great howl was heard from Haunted Mansion fans across the globe. Disney, in a nod to this guest-inspired story and legend, created a more realistic ring and embedded it into the new interactive queue line. Can you find it? It's on the ground near the base of a short brick pillar on the other side of the brick wall behind the busts for The Twins, Wellington & Forsythia. Photo courtesy of WDWGuidedTours.com

A Ghoulish Storm

As you journey through The Haunted Mansion, you'll notice its storyline takes place during a storm. Guests who visit the attraction at night will also notice that the same storm which thunders in scenes inside is carried outside as lightning periodically flashes and thunder rumbles across the mansion's facade. Perhaps that's why the ground is wet in the photo above!

MADAME LEOTA IS HAVING A BALL

Disney Imagineers are always innovating, and they added a fun twist to a Magic Kingdom classic, the tombstones at the Haunted Mansion.

Step into the queue line and move to the front outside the main entrance doors. To your left, you'll spot a number of tombstones, each with a witty epitaph paying tribute to one of the designers, developers and artists who originally created the attraction. However, one tombstone, which honors the late Imagineer Leota Toombs Thomas, is unlike any other. Keep an eye on it and you'll soon notice the face will begin to "stretch" and move. Suddenly, the eyes open, look around and then close, often frightening those who are caught unaware!

Her epitaph reads:

DEAR SWEET LEOTA
BELOVED BY ALL
IN REGIONS BEYOND NOW
BUT HAVING A BALL

Leota Toombs Thomas was a Disney Imagineer who worked creating attraction figures, such as the animals for The Jungle Cruise, the birds of The Enchanted Tiki Room, and the ghosts of the Haunted Mansion. As an homage to Leota, Disney Imagineers chose to use her face as the image of the disembodied head within the crystal ball in the Haunted

Mansion's seance scene, hence the reference on her tombstone to her "having a ball". Noted Disney voice talent Eleanor Audley provides the voice. Photos courtesy of WDWGuidedTours.com

"START TO SHRIEK AND HARMONIZE"

The quintet of singing busts in the lively graveyard scene, the ones singing "Grim Grinning Ghosts"? They all have names, and they are, from left to right, Rollo Rumkin, Uncle Theodore, Cousin Algernon, Ned Nub and Phineas P. Pock.

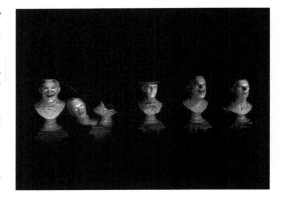

Note: Some guests incorrectly assume the "Uncle Theodore" bust is of Walt Disney, but it is actually of Thurl Ravenscroft, who had a bit of a resemblance to Walt. You can hear Mr. Ravenscroft's voice in many Disney productions and attractions, including Pirates of the Caribbean, The Enchanted Tiki Room and, of course, the Haunted Mansion. Photo courtesy of WDWGuidedTours.com

www.Disney-Secrets.com

YOUR THREE
NEW GHOUL FRIENDS

The names of the three hitchhiking ghosts at the end of the attraction?. . . Phineas, Ezra and Gus.

HAUNTED MANSION
PET CEMETERY

When exiting The Haunted Mansion, most guests make the mistake of passing too quickly by the wall at the mausoleum and the pet cemetery. Take a moment to stop and enjoy a ghoulish delight while others are  rushing off to the next attraction.

In the early 1980s, Disney Imagineer Kim Irvine, daughter of Leota Toombs Thomas, had the idea of using the rarely-seen side lawn of Disneyland's Haunted Mansion as a pet cemetery. Using off-the-shelf statuary, she worked with fellow Imagineer Chris Goosman to adorn each tombstone with witty epitaphs for such beloved pets as "Miss Kitty", "Bully" and "Big Jake". This new addition proved to be very popular with guests, so much so that Walt Disney Imagineering decided to add a larger pet cemetery in the front yard of the Haunted Mansion in 1993, where it has been light-heartedly haunting guests ever since. Realizing the 999 ghosts at Walt Disney World cared for their beloved pets, as well, the Imagineers brought this story element to the Magic Kingdom's Haunted Mansion where it resides on a hill behind a wrought iron fence. Photo courtesy of WDWGuidedTours.com

I'd like to thank Disneyland Haunted Mansion historian Jeff Baham, author of *The Unauthorized Story of Walt Disney's Haunted Mansion,* for this story.

BIG JAKE AND ROVER

Within the pet cemetery guests will find a tombstone for Rover, a faithful dog who passed away in 1898, well over 100 years ago. His epitaph reads...

Every Dog Has His Day
Too Bad Today is Your Day

If you're thinking the tombstone for Rover looks familiar, you're right, as here the Imagineers have chosen to place a tombstone which is nearly identical, though not exactly, to the tombstone found for another dog, Big Jake, at Disneyland's Haunted Mansion. Though 3,000 miles apart, these two tombstones eerily bookend the Magic Kingdom and Disneyland pet cemeteries.

LET THIS SECRET SINK IN

Those tombstones aren't leaning because of neglect on the Imagineers' part, they're leaning that way on purpose. As the story goes, each tombstone was standing straight on the day it was placed, but as the coffin below began to *deteriorate and decompose* the ground began to give way, causing the tombstones to settle and lean.

www.Disney-Secrets.com

ONE WILD RIDE TOO MANY?

Throughout the Magic Kingdom, guests will find Disney Imagineers have hidden small tributes to former attractions. Stop and look carefully at the pet cemetery and notice a small statue of Mr. Toad way in the back. This was placed  as a tribute to a Fantasyland attraction which is "no longer with us", Mr. Toad's Wild Ride. Photo courtesy of WDWGuidedTours.com

WATCH WHERE YOU STEP

 This next secret, while a tribute to Disney's attention to detail, is one countless guests have walked right over without ever knowing it existed, though they may wish they did!

During America's colonial period, buildings lacked today's modern plumbing amenities, including toilets. As such, people would pour their chamber pots containing waste matter out into the street gutters in front of their homes and businesses. Because there were no storm drains during this era, the waste would mix with rainwater and flow out into the unpaved streets. The brown "rivers" guests see winding their way down the middle of the streets throughout Liberty Square are a historically accurate nod to this unpleasant element of colonial life. Photo courtesy of WDWGuidedTours.com

THE LIBERTY TREE

This next secret actually reflects an idea from early Disneyland. Soon after Disneyland opened, Walt had an idea for a new "Land" just off the Town Square, called "Liberty Street". Representing Colonial

America, it would feature shops, restaurants and exhibits of the year 1775, and in the middle of its square would be a large oak tree adorned with 13 lanterns, each representing the original 13 colonies. Unfortunately, Walt never built Liberty Street in Disneyland, but the Disney Imagineers brought the idea for The Liberty Tree, as well as other ideas from Liberty Street, to the Magic Kingdom, where guests enjoy them today.

Note: The Liberty Tree in Liberty Square is a nearly 150 year-old live oak which was transplanted from another location at Walt Disney World Resort. Its acorns are used by Disney landscaping engineers to grow saplings for other areas in the park.

THE LIBERTY BELL

Found near the Liberty Tree is a life-sized replica of the historic Liberty Bell, the original of which hangs today in the Liberty Bell Center in Independence National Historical Park in Philadelphia, Pennsylvania.

Around the top of the bell are the words...

PROCLAIM LIBERTY THROUGHOUT ALL THE LAND UNTO ALL THE INHABITANTS THEREOF LEV. XXV. V X – BY ORDER OF THE ASSEMBLY OF THE PROVINCE OF PENSYLVANIA FOR THE STATE HOUSE IN PHILAD.A

Astute guests will notice that the word "Pensylvania" appears to be misspelled on the bell. However, this isn't a mistake, but instead it's another example of Disney's level of attention to historical detail found throughout Liberty Square.

So how did this spelling come about originally?

In 1751, the Pennsylvania Assembly sought to obtain a large bell that could be heard all throughout the small but growing town of Philadelphia, as the current bell, purportedly brought to America by William Penn and hung in a tree outside the meeting place of the Pennsylvania colonial assembly, was proving to be too small to be heard to the town's limits when rung. In turn, the Assembly commissioned London's Whitechapel Bell Foundry to cast the new bell, which was to be known as the Pennsylvania State House Bell. Messrs. Isaac

Norris, Thomas Leech and Edward Warner all signed the commission for the bell and directed that it should be "...shipped with the following words well shaped in large letters round it viz"...

BY order of the Assembly of the Province of Pensylvania for the State house in the City of Philad.a 1752 - Proclaim Liberty thro' all the Land to all the inhabitants thereof Levit. XXV. 10.

So at the hand of Messers. Norris, Leech and Warner the spelling of Pensylvania with only two "n"s originated, as this was considered to be an acceptable spelling of the word at that time.

Shortly after the bell's arrival in Philadelphia, it was discovered that the bell had suffered a crack, either in transit to America or upon its first ringing. Instead of having the bell shipped back to the Whitechapel Foundry, the Pennsylvania Assembly commissioned two Philadelphia men, John Pass and John Stow, to create an entirely new bell using the metal of the original one. Lacking the proper facilities of the Whitechapel Foundry, the two men broke the original bell into smaller pieces, melted them down and then recast the new bell with a similar design, though with a slightly different inscription, which read:

PROCLAIM LIBERTY THROUGHOUT ALL THE LAND UNTO ALL THE INHABITANTS THEREOF LEV. XXV. V X – BY ORDER OF THE ASSEMBLY OF THE PROVINCE OF PENSYLVANIA FOR THE STATE HOUSE IN PHILAD.A

PASS AND STOW
PHILAD.A
MDCCLIII

Upon the new bell's completion, it was hung in the tower of the State House, later known as Independence Hall. However, the citizens did not like the tone of the new bell at all, so they requested Pass and Stow recast the bell once again. The second casting was a success, and it was this second bell that would go on to become known worldwide as the Liberty Bell.

It is interesting to note that many Liberty Bell replicas make the claim that they were cast from the same mold as the original Liberty Bell of either 1751 or 1752. However, this is highly unlikely, as bells manufactured in the mid-1700s were cast using fragile molds made of clay, horse hair, loam and horse manure, and in the case of the Pass and Stow bell, the mold using these elements was formed within a hole dug into the ground. Because the original 1751 bell and the ensuing Pass and Stow bell of 1752 had not achieved historical significance at the time of their casting, it is highly unlikely that much thought would have been given at the time to keeping either of these original fragile molds, let alone arranging to have them preserved for well over 200 years so they may be used in the 20th century. If this were to have occurred, then these same molds would still be preserved today, yet the molds, or even photos of them, do not exist.

Part of the confusion arises from a number of replicas made of the 1752 Pass and Stow bell. In 1950, President Harry Truman created a savings bond campaign to pay for the casting of approximately 56 Liberty Bell replicas by the Paccard Fonderie in Annecy Le Vieux, France. These replicas were from

22 New Liberty Bell Replicas – 1950 – Paccard Fonderie, France

all new molds, using the Pass and Stow Liberty Bell as a *guide*, and because they were created by the large and well-equipped Paccard Foundry in 1950 instead of two men in a small foundry in 1752, the bells exhibited a more polished and refined exterior, differing greatly from the somewhat crude and rough exterior of the original Pass and Stow Liberty Bell. Guests will notice that the Liberty Square Liberty Bell, which was cast in 1989, reflects the more refined exterior of its contemporary casting.

Source: Interview with Robert Giannini III – Museum Curator – Independence National Historical Park – Philadelphia, PA

"The Liberty Bell of Independence National Historical Park: A Special History Study – John C. Paige.

Liberty Bell photo courtesy of WDWGuidedTours.com

HISTORICAL FIRE PROTECTION

If you make your way down a short alleyway between the Columbia Harbour House and the Hall of Presidents, you'll find affixed above two large garage doors an interesting plaque consisting of four hands grasping wrists set on a wooden shield. More than just a piece of art, this is another reflection of the Imagineers' attention to historical detail.

During the mid-1700s, building owners in Philadelphia could purchase fire insurance and, in turn, receive a "fire mark" such as this, which they would then affix on the exterior of their building, between the first and second floor. Upon completing their fire fighting efforts, volunteer fire departments would then bill the insurance company depicted on the fire mark.

Note: This fire mark belongs to Philadelphia's first fire insurance company, the Philadelphia Contributionship.

They Came By Sea

A famous moment in American history is captured in the details of the façade of the Hall of Presidents. If you look up at a second-story window facing towards the Haunted Mansion, you'll find two lanterns placed by Paul Revere to announce "One if by land, two if by sea."

The Windows Tell a Story

In yet another example of the Imagineers' attention to historical detail, study the nearby windows to find two items which reflect a common practice of the era. In one window you will find a cloth doll, which is there to notify firefighters that a child resides inside, and in a second floor window, you will spot a musket, signifying a minuteman soldier lives there and is at the ready to fight.

Clearly More Imagineering Detail

Now notice the number of small windows found throughout Liberty Square. As with Frontierland and Main Street, U.S.A., these windows reflect the Imagineers' commitment to the architecture and period-specific construction techniques available at the time these Lands represent. Contrary to the single larger panes of glass used throughout Tomorrowland, the windows here are small and many, as the ability to produce and transport large and expensive panes of glass wasn't available during the colonial period.

Now take a look at the construction technique used with each window. Notice how the Imagineers chose not to use modern window framing methods, but instead chose to use old-fashioned techniques by installing these windows using hand-applied window glazing, or putty. In nearby Frontierland, where supplies such as window glazing were difficult to come by in the old west, the windows are instead typically held in place with simple wood framing.

Clearly the Imagineers were dedicated to the period-specific details.

LIBERTY SQUARE RIVERBOAT

This next secret reveals how you can have a unique Magic Kingdom moment, which few guests get to experience.

Board the Liberty Square Riverboat and ask a Cast Member if you may join the Captain in the wheelhouse. There's a very good chance you'll be granted permission to do so. Then make your way mid-deck and open the door which leads to the Captain's Quarters.

Inside, you'll discover a fascinating area of the ship rarely seen by guests.

Now make your way up the narrow stairs and join the Captain as he pilots the grand ship down the Rivers of America. Be sure to ask to pull the cord which sounds the Liberty Belle's iconic steam whistle.

In addition, ask about receiving an official Riverboat Co-Pilot's license given to guests who help the Captain steer the grand vessel.

AN ALL NEW PERSPECTIVE

This next secret, while simple, is one which many guests miss because they think it's only a "boat ride", but it's far more than that.

Board the Liberty Square Riverboat and find a place on the front railing of the top deck. From here, you'll experience The Haunted Mansion, Frontierland, Big Thunder Mountain Railroad, Tom Sawyer Island and more from an entirely new and moving perspective.

You will also see story elements tucked along the shore which can be seen only from the Liberty Belle, something all the "landlubbers" will never experience!

YE OLDE CHRISTMAS SHOPPE

A stop inside the Ye Olde Christmas Shoppe reveals not one, but three different shops, each owned and decorated by a different colonial family; A woodcarver's family, a musician's family and a German family named Kepple, an homage to Walt Disney's grandfather, Kepple Disney.

A COMMITMENT TO DETAIL

Now take a moment to notice the address numbers, hinges and other ornamentation on the buildings of Liberty Square for another subtle and often overlooked attention to detail. It would've been far easier for Disney Imagineers to simply install modern day address numbers, hinges and such, but instead they chose to go the extra distance by installing items with the rough textured look of actual forged iron.

CHAPTER EIGHT

SECRETS OF FANTASYLAND

"Here is the world of imagination, hopes, and dreams. In this timeless land of enchantment, the age of chivalry, magic, and make-believe are reborn – and fairy tales come true. Fantasyland is dedicated to the young-in-heart, to those who believe that when you wish upon a star, your dreams come true."

- Walt Disney

TOWERING CINDERELLA CASTLE

Cinderella Castle is an excellent example of the forced perspective Disney Imagineers use to make it seem much taller than its 189-foot height. If guests look closely, they'll notice the scale of the architectural elements and stonework get much smaller as the eye leads higher. For example, the dimensions of the stones at the base of the castle are larger than those up higher, and the railings used at the top of the spire are only two feet tall, a full one and a half feet lower than other railings used throughout the parks.

THE DISNEY COAT OF ARMS

Before journeying through Cinderella Castle, take a moment to find the Coat of Arms posted over the front and rear entrances. With three lions passant in pale, (arranged vertically, with their right forepaws raised) these are the Coat of Arms for the Disney family. Photo courtesy of WDWGuidedTours.com

CINDERELLA'S FRIENDS

Observant guests will also notice the two mice watching from above at the receiving line area of Cinderella's Royal Table. They're friends of Cinderella, and their names are Jaq and Gus, from the beloved 1950 animated Disney film, "Cinderella."

A TRIBUTE TO TWO IMAGINEERS

From the windows on Main Street, U.S.A. to the tombstones of the Haunted Mansion, there are tributes to Disney Imagineers all around you as you travel throughout the Magic Kingdom. Here's one countless guests pass by each day without ever realizing it. Step into the passageway beneath Cinderella Castle and find the tile mural of Cinderella trying on the glass slipper. The two subjects at her feet are not fictional characters, but instead portray two actual Disney Imagineers; theme park and character designer John Hench (standing) and noted Disney artist and illustrator Herb Ryman.

MAD ABOUT THE DETAILS

Now find the images of Cinderella's two stepsisters in that scene, Anastasia and Drizella. Look closely and you'll notice the artist painstakingly portrayed their faces with green and red tiles to reflect them being green with envy and red with rage.

THE ROYALTY OF CINDERELLA

Upon exiting Cinderella Castle and entering Fantasyland, look to the left to discover a small fountain and statue of Cinderella with a bird alight on her hand. A curtsey to the princess reveals a crown placed upon her head, depicted by the painted mural behind her. It is interesting to note, however, that Cinderella is never portrayed in Disney films or stories as wearing a crown. Perhaps this scene is to indicate her position as royalty?

SIGHT TINKER BELL IN KEEP

"Wishes" is the spectacular fireworks performance which lights up the night sky in a dramatic pyrotechnic display scored to classic Disney songs high above Cinderella Castle. As the fireworks explode, guests suddenly realize Tinker Bell has taken flight to soar across the sky in a costume of brightly illuminated colors. It's a magical and daring addition to the "Wishes" nighttime spectacular.

Prior to Tinker Bell's flight, and while all the other guests' eyes are attracted to the dramatic fireworks, study the highest balcony atop the tallest keep (tower) of Cinderella Castle and you'll notice Tinker Bell standing in the dark while preparing for her flight.   Shortly after the first fireworks begin to explode, she begins to brilliantly glow and takes flight to the amazement of everyone below!

A GOODNIGHT
WISH FROM CINDERELLA

This next secret is one the vast majority of guests miss, yet it unveils a captivating magical moment in the Magic Kingdom.

Each day, guests hurry out of the park in order to be gone by the published park closing time.   It can be a bit of a hurried experience as they rush to catch their transportation back to their resort.   However, unknown to many, guests actually have one hour after the published closing time in which to make their way towards Main Street, U.S.A. and the exits.   During this "twilight hour," make your way towards Cinderella Castle, find a bench and take a moment to watch as it slowly adorns itself in a variety of constantly changing colors while saying goodnight to another enchanting day in the Magic Kingdom.   This is also one of the best times of the day in which to capture photos of Cinderella Castle, Tomorrowland and Main Street, U.S.A., as each is lit in a variety of colors and very few guests are in the foreground.

Tip: Think you'll somehow miss your bus and have to walk back to your hotel if you stay too long at the Magic Kingdom? Rest assured...Disney buses run up to two hours after the park closes, and the final bus is not allowed to leave until the park is cleared of all guests and the final OK is given by Security.

PRINCE CHARMING
REGAL CARROUSEL

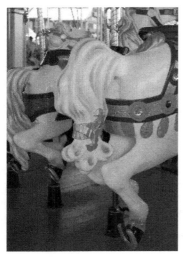

Now make your way towards the Prince Charming Regal Carrousel to find Cinderella's favorite carrousel horse.

Originally built in 1917, the Prince Charming Regal Carrousel (formerly Cinderella's Golden Carrousel) started its life as "Liberty" at Detroit Place Garden Park. In time, it was refurbished and moved to Olympic Park in Maplewood, New Jersey, before it was purchased by Disney in 1967 in anticipation of the opening of Walt Disney World Resort. It was restored by Walt Disney Imagineers and has been enjoyed by park guests since opening day on October 1, 1971.

There are 86 horses on the Prince Charming Regal Carrousel, but only one has any kind of ornamentation on its tail. Park legend has it the horse with the gold ribbon on its tail is Cinderella's favorite.

Tip: Guests have only a short time to pick and mount a horse once they are allowed onto the attraction, so knowing what Cinderella's favorite horse looks like *before* you get on the carrousel will help you find it quickly once your turn to ride comes, as well as help prevent any possible meltdowns involving young guests. The way to do so is to watch the carrousel horses before you get in line so as to learn how to spot Cinderella's favorite horse when you board the attraction.

A Hidden Nautilus

As you make your way through the standby queue for Under the Sea - Journey of The Little Mermaid, you'll find a tribute to the attraction which used to occupy this space in the form of a Hidden Mickey, or in this case, a Hidden Nautilus. Cleverly carved into the stonework on the left side before the water fountains is an image of the Nautilus, Jules Verne's futuristic submarine featured in both the 1954 Disney classic, "20,000 Leagues Under the Sea", as well as the former Fantasyland attraction.

A Hidden Tribute

Stand outside the exit for Peter Pan's Flight, and you'll notice a large wooden barrel off to one side labeled "Lost Boys Fire Brigade", along with the name of the Fire Chief. As with the windows which line Main Street, U.S.A., this barrel pays tribute to someone who plays an important role at Walt Disney World, the Fire Chief of the Reedy Creek Fire Department, the fire department charged with keeping all of Walt Disney World safe. However, unlike the windows of Main Street, U.S.A., the name painted on this barrel pays tribute to the *current* Fire Chief, and when this position changes hands, so does the name which appears on the barrel!

Note: The reason this barrel references the Lost Boys Fire Brigade is because it hides a fire hydrant.

REMEMBER...NOVEMBER 18TH

This next secret reveals a rare Hidden Mickey which appears only briefly once a year. As a result, very few guests ever get to see it. On the Under the Sea - Journey of The Little Mermaid attraction, Disney Imagineers cleverly included holes in the queue line rock formations which are aligned such that on November 18th...Mickey Mouse's birthday...the sun shines through to form a three-circle Hidden Mickey for only a few minutes right at noon. That's it above, shining at the base of the queue line wall. My thanks to Dave Drumheller of www.DigitalDisneyWorld.com for providing the perfectly timed photo.

Note: According to the Disney Archives, Mickey Mouse's birthdate "...has always been determined to be the date that Steamboat Willie opened at the Colony Theater.", which was November 18, 1928.

THE MANY ADVENTURES OF WINNIE THE POOH

Prior to the opening of The Many Adventures of Winnie the Pooh, the space was home to Mr. Toad's Wild Ride, a rollicking automobile adventure through the streets of London. As a tribute to this popular attraction, Disney Imagineers hung a picture in The Many Adventures of Winnie the Pooh of Mr. Toad handing the deed of this attraction to Owl. In addition, as if to recognize his "demise", they placed a statue of Mr. Toad in the pet cemetery of the Haunted Mansion.

SEVEN DWARFS MINE TRAIN

Disney Imagineers have carried on this tradition of honoring past attractions in one of the Magic Kingdom's newest attractions, the Seven Dwarfs Mine Train.

Near the mine's entrance, you'll spot a tall crane. Recognize those two vultures perched menacingly atop it? They are from the classic "dark ride" and guest favorite, "Snow White's Scary Adventures", which existed from the park's opening day on October 1, 1971 until May 31, 2012. It was closed as part of the extensive Fantasyland expansion, and the Snow White story is now portrayed in the exciting Seven Dwarfs Mine Train. In addition to these two characters, five of the Seven Dwarfs used in Snow White's Scary Adventures are also in the new attraction, and these are Bashful, Doc, Grumpy, Happy and Sleepy. Look for them in the cottage at the end of the ride, just before disembarking.

SIR MICKEY'S GIANT SECRET

He may be huge, but he's not easily seen. Stop in at Sir Mickey's Shop in Fantasyland and look up. There you'll find Willie the Giant from Mickey and the Beanstalk peeking in from under the roof.

"IT'S A SMALL WORLD"

Stop and enjoy the classic animated clock of "it's a small world" opposite the queue line as it puts on a show every quarter hour.

Chapter Nine

Secrets of Tomorrowland

"Tomorrow offers new frontiers in science, adventure, and ideals: the atomic age...the challenge of outer space...and the hope for a peaceful and unified world."

- Walt Disney

Buzz Lightyear's Space Ranger Spin

The next stop on the Secrets Tour brings you to the Winner's circle.

In the Buzz Lightyear's Space Ranger Spin attraction, guests compete against each other for the high score. It's fairly easy to rack up a *good* score, but if you want the big points and a chance to get to the coveted 999,999, then you have to know what to hit, as a handful of targets are worth 50,000 or 100,000 points each. Typically, the harder it is to hit the target, the more it's worth. Here are a few key targets...

- As you enter the room with the large orange robot, watch his right eye. (To your left) Once it begins blinking with an "X", it's worth 100,000 points.

- The menacing Zurg can be intimidating, but fire at a target at his base and you'll be rewarded with 100,000 points.

- Spot the volcano and fire on the target at the top. It is worth 50,000 points.

You have your mission, so blast away and help Buzz save the Galactic Empire from Evil Emperor Zurg! Photo courtesy of WDWGuidedTours.com

SPACE MOUNTAIN

Here's a tip which may give you a rare inside look at Space Mountain with the lights on.

If you're in Tomorrowland and Space Mountain is closed, chances are the lights are on inside as Imagineers are performing some maintenance on the tracks. Walk over to the nearby Tomorrowland Transit Authority, which usually has a very short wait time of five minutes or less, and climb aboard a transport vehicle. The vehicle traverses through Space Mountain, so you'll get an inside look at the attraction with the lights on as you travel along.

Note: Does Space Mountain in the Magic Kingdom look larger than its counterpart in Disneyland? That's because it is. Disneyland's Space Mountain is 200' in diameter, while the Magic Kingdom's comes in at 300'.

MONSTERS, INC. LAUGH FLOOR

This next secret has to do with being in the right place at the right time to be the right choice. During each performance of the Monsters, Inc. Laugh Floor, one person is selected from an audience of 400 guests to be "That Guy", someone the show highlights and teases repeatedly throughout the show, but all in a good-natured manner. For being a good sport, this one person is given a unique souvenir very few

guests ever receive, their very own "I was that guy at Monsters, Inc. Laugh Floor" sticker! Photo courtesy of WDWGuidedTours.com

ROBO-NEWZ

After you exit the Tomorrowland Transit Authority, wander over to the entrance to the Astro Orbiter and look for the "Robo-Newz" robot featuring "up-to-the-minute" news. While only a prop, this high-tech robot "offers" newspapers printed while you wait. The latest edition of the Galaxy Gazette sports a headline which reads, "Stitch Escapes!", a tie-in to the nearby "Stitch's Great Escape!"

METROPHONE

Now make your way to the nearby Metrophone. Brought to you by the Galactic Communications Network, this is a galactic phone booth offering toll free calls to anywhere in the galaxy. Make your selection on the dial and listen in on one of a few different interstellar calls!

A STYLING HIDDEN MICKEY

Hidden Mickeys are fun to spot anywhere, even in the future!

While you ride the Tomorrowland Transit Authority attraction, take note of the futuristic scene in which a woman is having her hair done while sitting with a large "styling device" over her entire head. Though somewhat difficult to see, if you study her belt, you'll see a classic 3-Circle Hidden Mickey.

SECRETS OF EPCOT
FUTURE WORLD

But the most exciting and, by far, the most important part of our Florida project, in fact, the heart of everything we'll be doing in Disney World, will be our experimental prototype city of tomorrow. We call it EPCOT, spelled E-P-C-O-T: Experimental Prototype Community of Tomorrow. Here it is in larger scale. EPCOT will take its cue from the new ideas and new technologies that are now emerging from the creative centers of American industry. It will be a community of tomorrow that will never be completed, but will always be introducing testing and demonstrating new materials and new systems. And EPCOT will always be a showcase to the world of the ingenuity and imagination of American free enterprise.

- Walt Disney

SPACESHIP EARTH

Epcot's Spaceship Earth attraction takes guests on a journey through time as they marvel at scenes depicting the advancement of communication technology over the ages, from the invention of papyrus for written communication between men to today's digital signals transmitted between planets.

In 2008, Spaceship Earth underwent a significant reimagineering, and as part of that Disney Imagineers wanted to represent the era of telegraphy, captured in a scene in which a telegraph operator transmits the historical news of the ceremonial driving of the Golden Spike near Promontory Summit, Utah on May 10, 1869, thus completing the Transcontinental Railroad. To "plus" the scene, the Imagineers decided to have the sound of the Morse Code being tapped out by the telegraph operator be audible to guests as they traveled by in their vehicles, and to ensure its accuracy, it was further decided that this Morse Code would be in "American Morse", or "Railroad Morse", as it was also known, as this was the type of Morse Code used in that part of the country at that point in time. However, this presented a problem when it came to finding someone today who could tap out that message, as American Morse became largely extinct in the early 1900s, being replaced by International Morse Code.

In considering their options, one of the Disney Imagineers, Glenn Barker, recalled a guest, Mr. George Eldridge, who had brought to his attention years before an error Mr. Eldridge had noticed in the Morse Code being tapped out for Walt Disney's Opening Day speech at the Disneyland Railroad New Orleans

Square Station. Using his skillful ear and modern day technology, Mr. Eldridge worked with Mr. Barker to correct the error.

Realizing Mr. Eldridge could probably help the Imagineers solve this current problem, Mr. Barker contacted him and asked for his assistance. After getting up to speed on American Morse Code, Mr. Eldridge tapped out the message you hear today in the Spaceship Earth attraction, thus making him perhaps the only guest to have his work featured in an attraction in both Disneyland and Walt Disney World!

The message you hear being tapped out in the Spaceship Earth telegraphy scene...

PROMONTORY UTAH
GOLDEN SPIKE
RR CPT
USA CONNECTED

Where "RR CPT" is the Railway Telegraph abbreviation for "Railroad Complete.

Source: My interview with Mr. George Eldridge

Note: If the scene in the Spaceship Earth attraction is depicting the actual telegrapher at the scene of the Golden Spike ceremony, then the name of the telegrapher is Watson Shilling.

www.Disney-Secrets.com

EAST MEETS WEST MEETS WALT

It's interesting to note that of the countless locomotive designs in use throughout history, the two steam locomotives used for the ceremonial driving of the Golden Spike at Promontory Summit, Utah were both similar in design to the Central Pacific #173, the steam locomotive which Walt Disney used as the inspiration for his miniature "Lilly Belle" steam engine, which he built and ran on his "Carolwood Pacific" railroad in the backyard of his Holmby Hills home. This miniature locomotive played an important role in Disney history and became the inspiration for all the train engines you see at Disney theme parks around the world today.

Above is a photo of Central Pacific #173, and below is a photo of a replica of one of the trains from the Golden Spike ceremony, the Jupiter, which is officially known as Central Pacific #60.

FOUNTAIN OF NATIONS

As guests make their way into Future World, they pass by the large Fountain of Nations. Performing a majestic display every 15 minutes, this fountain is unlike any other you'll ever see. Representing a world of inclusive harmony, its dedication ceremony in 1982 included representatives from 29 different nations pouring water from their countries into the fountain, with water from the Mississippi River representing the United States.

FUTURE WORLD EAST & FUTURE WORLD WEST

Here's a secret most guests walk through, around and over without ever noticing. As you make your way into Future World, stop and notice the subtle difference in the architectural and landscaped features between Future World East and Future World West. Future World East is a world of science and technology, and as such, the Imagineers conveyed this using construction with hard angles, straight pathways and geometrical features, whereas Future World West reflects more of the natural wonders of our planet, and this is represented in more free-flowing designs with softer edges, curved walkways and, of course, plenty of water.

www.Disney-Secrets.com

Jammin' at Epcot

Walk right past that group of janitors, and you may be making a big mistake.

When visiting Epcot, keep an eye out for a rather boisterous bunch of janitors. At first glance, it may appear they're simply on their way to do some cleaning, but stop and watch, because you're about to witness JAMMitors, a percussion group which mixes fast-paced percussion on trash cans with an interactive comedy filled performance. During Epcot's International Food & Wine Festival, you'll find this same group performing as the Jammin' Chefs on pots and pans over stoves.

Test Track

Motor over to Test Track Presented by Chevrolet and climb into your own custom test vehicle to experience a nearly mile-long attraction at close to 65 m.p.h.. . . making it the longest and fastest attraction

in all of Walt Disney World Resort.

Universe of Energy

When designing the Universe of Energy attraction, the Imagineers realized they had the opportunity to showcase leading-edge energy technologies. As a result, they built the attraction utilizing  80,000 photovoltaic cells. Located in solar panels on the roof, these cells produce 70,000 watts of direct current, or 15% of the power needed to run this attraction.

29 Landing Spots

 Journey to the entrance of Mission: SPACE and find the large model of the moon. There, on its surface, you'll find 29 indicators which represent the 29 different landing sites used by astronauts and unmanned spacecraft.

Soarin' Around the World

With the recent re-Imagineering of this attraction, Disney Imagineers gave guests two new Hidden Mickeys. The first appears briefly when three colorful hot air balloons align for only a moment near the center of the screen, while the second appears as fireworks burst above Epcot's Spaceship Earth.

THE SEAS WITH
NEMO & FRIENDS

Did you know you can snorkel with the fish, rays, sea turtles and even sharks of The Seas with Nemo & Friends? Disney offers the 2.5 hour "Epcot Seas Aqua Tour" for those guests who don't have open water SCUBA certification.

Want to take it to the next level? If you have open water SCUBA certification, you can also scuba dive at The Seas with Nemo & Friends by taking part in the 3-hour "DiveQuest" tour.

Would you believe you can also swim with dolphins at Walt Disney World?! You can with Disney's "Dolphins in Depth." This 3-hour tour allows guests to get up close and interact with dolphins in knee-deep water.

Learn more about these tours and make reservations by calling 407-939-8687.

THE LAND

In designing the entrance to THE LAND, the Imagineers wanted to convey to guests a sense of the bountiful, dynamic and powerful elements which make up our planet. Rows and rows of foliage and plants represent earth's natural riches and bounty, while trees flower in white to convey the essence of life giving weather in the sky, and the layers of earth folded and heaved under tremendous forces are captured in the tile mosaic at the entrance to the attraction.

THE WORLD'S LARGEST FLOWER BED

The immense flower bed you're walking by outside the entrance to The Land? It's the largest flower bed found in all of Walt Disney World Resort and holds 20,000 plants.

BEHIND THE SEEDS

Guests can actually "dig deeper" into The Land.

Don't miss the opportunity to go beyond the exhibits and take a close look at the four greenhouses, fish farm, high-tech horticulture and more going on behind the scenes. The "Behind the Seeds" greenhouse tour is an intriguing 45-minute journey behind closed doors in which you will take an herb and spice challenge, feed fish at the fish farm, release some ladybugs, see record setting plants and more. Same day reservations can be made at the Tour Desk on the lower level of The Land or by calling 407-WDW-TOUR (407-939-8687) in advance.

A RECORD TOMATO TREE

An official Guinness World Record holding secret is up next at The Land pavilion.

A voyage on the Living with the Land boat ride reveals a record setting tomato tree which weighs over 1,100 pounds and produces more than 32,000 tomatoes in one year! In addition to the world record tomato tree, guests will also find a cucumber tree, nine-pound lemons and Mickey Mouse shaped cucumbers, watermelons and pumpkins.

NONE OF THEIR BEESWAX

As you make your journey through Living with the Land, study the myriad plants, flowers, fruits and vegetables. Notice what's missing? It is an absolutely critical component required for plants to live, grow and thrive...yet you won't find it here. It's bees! Disney Imagineers knew that having guests floating through the attraction amidst thousands of busy bees could possibly create a problem, especially with those guests who are allergic to bee stings, so they created the attraction without them. The solution? Scientists spend about fifteen hours each week hand pollinating the plants, a process they've had to do since opening day.

Journey Into Imagination

Look closely during the Journey Into Imagination attraction and you'll see the Imagineers have hidden a reference to two classic Disney films amidst the props. The letterman's jacket with the letter "M", hanging in the computer lab, is a reference to Medfield College, the college at which The Absent Minded Professor taught in Disney's 1961 film by the same name.

While the tennis shoes, along with the names Dean Higgins, Professor Quigley and Dexter Riley on the wall nearby, are all references to Disney's 1969 movie, "The Computer Wore Tennis Shoes."

SECRETS OF EPCOT
WORLD SHOWCASE

"To all who come to this Place of Joy, Hope and Friendship, Welcome. EPCOT is inspired by Walt Disney's creative vision. Here, human achievements are celebrated through imagination, wonders of enterprise and concepts of a future that promises new and exciting benefits for all. May EPCOT Center entertain, inform and inspire, and, above all, may it instill a new sense of belief and pride in man's ability to shape a world that offers hope to people everywhere."

- Card Walker – Epcot Dedication

SHOWCASE PLAZA

Tucked to the right hand side of Showcase Plaza are two telescopes right at the water's edge, just waiting to show the world from an all new perspective.

While most guests enter World Showcase and rush off in the direction of either Mexico or Canada, those who break from the pack and proceed straight ahead will find an expansive view of World Showcase along with these two telescopes, which allow unique close up views of each pavilion from a single location.

ELEVEN AND THEN SOME

In addition to the eleven pavilions you see today, there were an additional eight pavilions considered before the park opened. These were the African Nations pavilion, Costa Rica, Denmark, Iran, Israel, Spain, Switzerland and Venezuela.

ILLUMINATIONS

While IllumiNations is a dramatic pyrotechnic spectacle for all of World Showcase Lagoon, it was purposely designed to look best from Showcase Plaza, for it is here the Earth Globe is centered for much of the show, as well as its dramatic finale. Getting access to this prime viewing spot takes some inside knowledge, coordination and timing, however. The entrance to this broad slightly sloped area is roped off until just 10 minutes prior to showtime when Cast Members allow guests to fill the area and take their seats on the ground. The area is then closed again 5 minutes before the spectacle begins. Note that guests are required to sit during the performance, as no standing is allowed.

Tip: If you want the best photos, you'll want to be at the very front. Note that there is a railing there.

SPECTACULAR DINING VIEW

The La Hacienda de San Angel restaurant at Epcot's Mexico pavilion is also an excellent place from which to enjoy IllumiNations. This restaurant was designed specifically to give guests an outstanding view of the fireworks spectacular during their dining. Reservations are encouraged.

ON WITH THE SHOW

Many guests incorrectly assume that IllumiNations will be cancelled if it's raining, or it looks like it's going to rain, but this is incorrect. IllumiNations is never cancelled due to rain, so if it looks like there is going to be some precipitation then stick around, as all kinds of excellent viewing spots will begin to open up as other guests leave.

Tip: IllumiNations will be cancelled due to high winds or if there is any lightning in the area, and the decision to cancel the performance is typically made shortly before its scheduled beginning. This is an important point to keep in mind if you are planning on leaving another park to head over to Epcot to see the show. If it is very windy or the possibility of lightning exists, then don't bother to make the trip.

KIDCOT FUN STOPS

When Epcot opened in 1982, the Imagineers soon realized its focus on science, technology and world attractions failed to generate the same kind of interest young children had in the Magic Kingdom, its characters and story elements. As a result, they began to develop new programs which would allow kids to interact with the park, and one of these was Kidcot Fun Stops, a journey filled with enchanting stops at each pavilion where children could decorate their own personal souvenir with the colors, trinkets and stamps of each country. Stop by a pavilion as you enter World Showcase and ask a Cast Member for a Kidcot Fun Stops souvenir.

MEXICO

Stop for a moment in front of the Mexico pavilion and study its tall pyramid for another example of the same forced perspective Disney Imagineers use with Cinderella Castle, Expedition Everest and Main Street, U.S.A. While it appears much higher, the pyramid's total height is less than 50 feet.

NORWAY

Before you duck into the small Kringla Bakeri Og Kafe, take note of the special roof the Imagineers were sure to include in the pavilion as a nod to a rather interesting piece of Norway's ancient heritage. While other  buildings in the pavilion are covered in stone, wood and tile, this small roof is made of sod.

Comprised of approximately three inches of sod and covering a thin layer of long-lasting birch bark, which makes the roof waterproof, this construction technique has been used since before the time of the Vikings, as ancient Norwegians realized that such a roof is not only inexpensive, but also an excellent insulator in both hot and cold weather.

Now take note of the little metal railing affixed to the gutter. In another attention to detail, this railing's purpose is to keep any snow and ice from sliding off the roof and onto guests below. It is Norway, after all!

TO AS EN

As you enter the Norway pavilion, take note of the rather interesting architectural feature shared by two buildings patterned after the colorful wooden houses of Bryggen, a historic harbour district in Bergen, Norway. There on the left are two gift shops selling crystal, ceramics and other fine Norwegian merchandise. While they are clearly two different buildings, as defined by the joining of their separate roofs, they share between them one common doorway, a unique architectural feature which is not uncommon in Bryggen.

Norway's Stave Church

The majestic building at the entrance to the Norway pavilion? It's a Stave Church based on the Gol Stave Church, which was originally built around 1212 A.D. in Hallingdal, Norway, and yes, you're more than welcome to step inside to learn all about the interesting history of the Vikings.

Before you do so, however, take note of the wooden statue out front. That is of Olaf Haraldsson, or "Saint Olaf", the Patron Saint of Norway.

Bricked Up Windows

Now continue past Norway's entrance area and find the round tower at the end of the pavilion, on the way to China. Study carefully the stone facade. Do you see the bricked up windows which do not match the stone? Surely the Disney Imagineers didn't make a mistake, which they then had to cover up, did they? No, not at all. This is another example of the Imagineers' attention to both detail and history.

Originating out of England's Lights and Windows tax of 1696, residents of Norway were in time assessed a tax based upon the number of windows in their home. Given glass was expensive, the tax assessors reasoned that the more windows in a residence, the more wealth and income the homeowner must have, so a tax on windows would not only be easy to determine, as one could simply count the windows from outside, but it would also be fair for all. However, Norwegians cleverly worked to evade this "window tax" by boarding or bricking up the windows they felt they could live without. In this case, it was the higher windows in the tower. Photo courtesy of WDWGuidedTours.com

HAT'S OFF TO A
CLASSIC THAT IS NO MORE

At one time, the Norway pavilion was home to the Maelstrom boat ride, as well as a Hidden Mickey known both far and wide. As with Disney Imagineers' practice of paying respects to former attractions, I've decided to keep a reference to it within this book, even though it has now set sail. As guests stood in the queue for Norway's Maelstrom boat ride, they would've noticed a Viking ship on the left side of a large mural which depicted the history and wonders of Norway. There, in the middle of a crowded ship, was a perfect example of Disney Imagineering whimsy, as amidst all the battle-ready warriors was one lone Viking wearing Mickey Mouse ears! And to top it all off, the name stitched on the front was "Leif". Truly classic.

CHINA

Now journey next door and see another attention to detail which is subtle, yet very important to an accurate portrayal of the host country.

Notice the water in the landscaping at the China pavilion. Here, as in China itself, water used in a landscape is typically still, whereas the water found in other pavilions, such as Japan or France, involves movement or flow.

PRINCE MIN

This next secret reveals a prince at Walt Disney World whom nobody has ever heard of, yet he's there to be seen by tens of thousands every day.

Venture to the China pavilion and find a small sculpture of a man atop a hen on the roofline of the Nine Dragons Restaurant. This man is Prince Min, a cruel 3rd century ruler who was hanged for his actions. His presence on the roof is a warning to all other tyrants to keep away, and the other animals behind him are there to keep him from escaping.

"Water Spouting Basin"

Now make your way towards the back of the China pavilion and step into the Yong Feng Shangdian shop. There, on a pedestal, is a large bronze basin with two handles, one which most guests assume to be a simple wash basin.  This basin, however, is unlike any you've ever seen before, as it is the Fish Basin, or "water-spouting" basin. The small sign above the basin reads...

"The fish basin is dated back to the song Dynasty (960 to 1279 A.D.). The bronze basin has two prominent handles and four fish in relief on the bottom, as well as a line emanating from the mouths or tails of the fish. When the handles are rubbed briskly with the palms of the hands, a harmonious sound is heard and standing waves are excited in the four quadrants along the circumference. Meanwhile water column comes alive, spouting into the air, as if squirting from the four fish."

Rubbing your palms lengthwise along the handles creates a resonation which quickly causes the water to "dance" in the four quadrants of the bowl. Note that rubbing your hands on the handles in a lateral outward and back motion does not create the same effect. Go ahead and give it a try!

Coolpost

Stop at the Coolpost between the China and Germany pavilions and lift the lids on the old-fashioned Coca-Cola coolers for a fun secret most guests walk right past.

GERMANY

As you enter the Germany pavilion, take notice of the façade of Das Kaufhaus to your right. Here the Imagineers have paid tribute to the historical Merchants' Hall of Freiburg im Breisgau in southwest Germany. Hundreds of years old  now and dating back to the 14th century, this impressive structure served as an important financial institution to the region.

Due to the space limitations of the Germany pavilion, the Imagineers elected to build this architectural replica approximately three-quarters the size of the original structure. As such, it is adorned with three statues, instead of the four found on the façade in Freiburg im Breisgau. But just who do these statues represent? They are a family of Monarchs and Emperors dating back to 1459! From left to right, you'll find...

Philip I of Castile

Born in July of 1478, Philip I of Castile, also known as Philip the Handsome, was the son of Emperor Maximilian I. Because he died before his father, he never became an emperor, but instead was the first Habsburg Monarch of Spain.

Emperor Charles V

Born in 1500, Charles V was the eldest son of Philip I of Castile. Becoming the ruler of the Netherlands at age 6, he ruled over a domain comprised of nearly four million square kilometers, ultimately assuming the role of Emperor from his grandfather, Maximilian I.

Ferdinand I

The younger brother of Charles V, Ferdinand I was born in March of 1503. As a Royal, he became King of Bohemia, Hungary and Croatia before becoming Emperor upon the death of his brother, Charles V, in 1558.

Missing from this collection of three statues is the father of all three, Emperor Maximilian I, whom is depicted on the original facade to the left of all three.

Note: The small ornate item above each statue's head is called a baldachin. Photo courtesy of WDWGuidedTours.com

A ROYAL HIDDEN MICKEY

In another example of Imagineering whimsy, study the three statues adorning Das Kaufhaus and find the one sporting a crown with a Hidden Mickey front and center. Tip: You may find it easier to zoom in with your camera, which will allow you to study the detail of the crown.

St. George

While in the Germany pavilion, it's impossible to miss the dramatic statue in the middle of the platz. Here the Imagineers have paid tribute to St. George, the patron saint of soldiers, who slayed a dragon which was about to take the life of a King's daughter. Statues and artwork conveying this same story can be found all throughout Germany, and while all vary in their appearance and interpretation, all are quite impressive.

A Chime to Remember

If you pass through the Germany pavilion too quickly, you'll most likely miss this next secret. Each hour, on the hour, the large glockenspiel, located beneath the clock at the back of the platz, or plaza, performs a unique chime composed especially for the pavilion, complete with two charming Hummel figurines who emerge from under an ornate baldachin and strike a large bell.

ITALY

This next secret reveals again the Imagineers' commitment to detail and quality, even when it cannot be viewed up close by guests.

The Italy pavilion features a stunning replica of the historical bell tower of Saint Mark's Basilica in Venice, Italy, and high atop the campanile (the bell tower) is a beautiful golden statue of the Archangel Gabriel, painstakingly sculpted to match the original. Those guests wishing to get a closer look at this statue may view a nearly exact replica of this replica while touring the gardens within the Italy pavilion.

THE AMERICAN ADVENTURE

Every one of Walt Disney World's theme parks have what Walt Disney called a "weenie", a prominent icon which beckons guests to draw closer. Most are readily apparent...in the Magic Kingdom it's Cinderella Castle, and in Disney's Animal Kingdom it's the

Tree of Life. Spaceship Earth is Epcot's "weenie", but there is also another weenie hidden by distance. Stand at Showcase Plaza and gaze across World Showcase Lagoon. There on the opposite shore standing proud is The American Adventure pavilion, the weenie for World Showcase.

Initially, Disney Imagineers thought of placing The American Adventure pavilion at the entrance to World Showcase as a way to convey that America was welcoming guests to the world. However, Dick Nunis, Disney's Chief of Operations for all the parks, stated it should be on the far shore of World Showcase Lagoon so as to encourage guests to walk around the promenade. According to Marty Sklar, in his book, "Dream It! Do It!", Dick Nunis stated..."*We have to give our guests a key reason to go all the way around that big lagoon.*"..."*We need to put the big attraction - like the castle of the Magic Kingdom - at the far side of the lagoon to make people want to go there!*"

AMERICA...STANDING TALLER THAN YOU THINK

Now take a moment to study another example of Disney's use of forced perspective. Standing in front of The American Adventure, you'll notice, by the placement and size of the doors and windows, that it appears to be only a two-story building, which was the limit in this colonial period due to available building technology. However, stand someone next to the building to give it proper scale and you'll discover it is actually 4 to 5 stories tall!

OWN A PIECE OF THE AMERICAN ADVENTURE

As with the wallpaper of the Haunted Mansion, the Disneyland Rose, the Mickey Mouse Plant or even the Asepso soap Hidden Mickey box, many guests enjoy owning a part of the Disney theme parks to have at home, and this next secret adds one more item to the list. Two, actually!

Take note of the scene in The American Adventure of the four men on the porch of the Depression era gas station. There on the wall, behind the banjo player, are two WPA era posters showcasing Great Smoky Mountains National Park and Fort Marion National Monument in St. Augustine, Florida. Both of these impressive posters are available for purchase through www.RangerDoug.com.

"Ranger Doug" is actually Doug Leen, a former seasonal Park Ranger who, in 1973, began leading the effort to rescue, restore and replicate the rare National Park posters which were produced under the WPA, beginning on August 26, 1938.

Note: The 1938 printing of the first of these posters by the WPA dates this porch scene to 1938 or later.

If you visit the Ranger Doug web site above, you'll find a very interesting history about these unique posters. Photo courtesy of WDWGuidedTours.com.

Japan

Stately in its presence, a five story pagoda welcomes guests to the Japan pavilion. Modeled after the 8th century Horyuji Temple in Nara, Japan, its architecture is more than simple form, function or design, but instead specifically represents a connection with the earth and heavens. Each of its five layers represent, in ascending order, Earth, Water, Fire, Wind and Heaven.

World Showcase Lagoon Tides

This next secret is very subtle, yet adds a great deal to the story that is the Japan pavilion. Disney Imagineers, knowing World Showcase Lagoon is an enclosed body of water lacking tidal movement, added barnacles at the base of the large torii gate at the Japan waterfront to give guests a realistic impression of tidal movements in a salt-water environment.

Attracting Good Luck

Now turn from the torii gate and study the rooflines of the buildings in the Japan pavilion. Look carefully and you'll notice some are adorned with large golden fish. It is a belief in Japan that storks nesting on roofs bring good luck and happiness to the family inhabiting the building, so ornamental fish are often placed atop roofs to attract storks.

Morocco

A stop at Morocco can sometimes reveal one of children's favorite Disney characters. Journey far towards the back of the Morocco pavilion, turn a corner and step inside a doorway adorned with a Mickey Mouse hand to look for  Aladdin, who sometimes "flies" in on his carpet to greet guests, sign autograph books and have a picture taken.

Note: Study the mural of the street scene backdrop and you'll find a Hidden Mickey! Hint: It's on the right side of the street.

Photo courtesy of WDWGuidedTours.com

A CLASSIC HIDDEN MICKEY

Out front, at the Sauk-Al-Magreb Gifts of Morocco, guests will find one of Epcot's most notable Hidden Mickeys. Take a moment to study the marketplace on the Showcase Lagoon side of the Morocco pavilion and find three plates arranged in a classic Hidden Mickey design. They may be moved periodically and change in appearance from time to time, but they're always there.

MOROCCO PAVILION TOURS

Many secrets at Walt Disney World reveal themselves with just a single inquiry. "Why do you suppose this is here?", "What is the meaning of that?" and "Is there more than meets the eye?" Unfortunately, countless secrets are missed by guests each day because they, like many of us, are in a hurry to see the next amazing sight. This next secret is available to anyone just for the asking.

The Morocco pavilion offers guests a rare opportunity to go beyond the facades and further immerse themselves in the rich culture of Morocco. Three times each day, Moroccan cultural ambassadors take guests on a guided 20 to 45 minute tour of the pavilion to explore all about the Moroccan culture, history, architecture, people and more. To learn about this tour, stop by the Moroccan National Tourist Office at the pavilion.

FRANCE

Forced perspective is an important story element used throughout Walt Disney World Resort, and the France pavilion's Eiffel Tower is another excellent example of its use.

As an iconic image of France, Disney Imagineers had no choice but to include the Eiffel Tower as part of the France pavilion, but they were faced with a bit of a problem. The Eiffel Tower's overwhelming size obviously would not fit within the pavilion, so they planned to construct a replica of the tower which was one-tenth the size of the original. However, they realized that guests viewing this replica up close would simply consider it to be an oversized model, so to solve this problem and to give the tower a sense of majestic height and distance, the Imagineers used forced perspective from top to bottom and placed the Eiffel Tower such that guests could not see its base. This creates the illusion the tower is as large as the original and approximately one mile away.

FRENCH ATTENTION TO DETAIL

As you leave the France pavilion and head over the bridge to the United Kingdom, take a moment to move from the crowd and peer over both sides of the bridge railings to find more examples of the Disney Imagineers'

attention to detail and storytelling.

A rare first edition post-WWII issue of Le Journal de Mickey – Author's personal collection

UNITED KINGDOM

The largest secret at the United Kingdom pavilion literally surrounds guests as they walk its streets. Each of the buildings' facades and interiors represent a period of time, beginning with The Tea Caddy and its

thatched roof representing the 1500s. The Queen's Table, the two-story building with diamond shaped wooden moldings, clovers and chevrons, denotes the 1600s, while its Queen Anne Room represents the 1700s, and the Lords and Ladies façade captures the architecture of the 1800s.

A CANTILEVERED SECRET

Now take a moment to study the architecture near The Queen's Table. Notice how each ascending story is cantilevered above the previous story? In the period these buildings represent, taxes assessed on a building were based upon the square footage of the first floor. As a result, building owners sought to minimize the tax they owed by constructing buildings with a first floor having a narrow and small footprint, while ensuing floors were built larger and overhanging the first.

A SPORTY HIDDEN MICKEY

The sign hanging above the entrance to the Sportsman's Shoppe holds a Hidden Mickey. Can you find it?

A Dignified Secret

On the entrance sign to the Rose & Crown pub, you'll find the Latin phrase, "Otium cum Dignitate". Is it the royal dictate of a notable king? The battle cry of a decorated General? Perhaps the motto of oppressed servants? Actually, none of the above. It means "Leisure with Dignity." Fittingly adorning a pub, it refers to leisurely pursuits in retirement after a life of hard work.

Leisurely Enjoying the View

"Leisure with Dignity" is practiced with this next secret. Instead of walking past the UK Pavilion, step behind The Tea Caddy to find a collection of benches tucked amidst a colorful perennial garden, home to butterflies and a captivating view of World Showcase.

Tip: Want to know one of the best places to watch Illuminations? It's from Epcot's UK pavilion. Get there early, as seating is somewhat limited. Also be mindful of which way the wind is blowing, because if it's blowing your way, the smoke from the performance will obscure your view, so you'll want to be upwind on the other side of World Showcase Lagoon.

CANADA

The Canada pavilion employs two excellent examples of forced perspective. The Rocky Mountains above Victoria Gardens and the stately five-story Hotel du Canada, each designed to appear much higher than they actually are. Study the Hotel du Canada and take note of how the size of the lowest windows are much larger than those at the base of its Mansard roof.

BUTCHART GARDENS INSPIRATION

The "Victoria Gardens" are inspired by the world-famous Butchart Gardens near Victoria, British Columbia.

A Canadian Hidden Mickey

As you reach the top of the stairs at the entrance to the Canada pavilion, look for the large Totem Pole to the left. Study it carefully, and you'll discover a classic 3-Circle Hidden Mickey.

SECRETS OF DISNEY'S HOLLYWOOD STUDIOS

"The World you have entered was created by The Walt Disney Company and is dedicated to Hollywood – not a place on the map, but a state of mind that exists wherever people dream and wonder and imagine, a place where illusion and reality are fused by technological magic. We welcome you to a Hollywood that never was – and always will be."

- Michael Eisner - Disney's Hollywood Studios Dedication

MUPPET-VISION 3D

The Muppets are a quirky and colorful collection of characters constantly engaged in well-intentioned chaos and mayhem. Disney Imagineers have captured this spirit and worked to convey it from the very moment guests enter the attraction...and this is where you'll find the first secret...

UNLOCK THIS MUPPET SECRET

As you enter the Muppet-Vision 3D attraction, you'll find a fun secret which is missed by thousands of guests every day. Just as you pass through the turnstiles, look to your right and you'll find a sign

hanging in the window which reads, "Back in 5 Minutes. *Key is under Mat.*" Go ahead and lift the mat!

AN HOMAGE TO A FAMOUS MOUSKETEER

The next Walt Disney World secret is more for mom and dad. As you enter the staging area for the Muppet Vision 3-D attraction, you'll notice "a net full of Jell-O" hanging from the ceiling on the left and towards the back.

Ponder this, and you'll realize this is a nod to Annette Funicello, perhaps the most famous of all Mouseketeers.

A GREAT HIDDEN MICKEY

After exiting the attraction, take a moment to study the fountain out front. Find Gonzo the Great, and you will have found a "Muppetized" Hidden Mickey.

A SECRET SUNDAE

Now make your way to the exterior of the attraction, just to the right of the entrance. There you will find several large concrete planters atop a high wall. Take a look at the "planter" in the back and you'll notice it's unlike all the others in that it's an empty sundae dish containing an oversized spoon!

PIPE DOWN, GONZO

The Muppet Vision 3-D attraction is filled with all kinds of quirky signs and messages inside and out. While by the oversized sundae, find the large pipe turned downward and you will have found the Imagineers' playful tribute to Gonzo the Great. Of course, the pipe represents Gonzo's nose!

Catch Gonzo In Time

This next secret is for those who are looking down at their phones or are unaware of their surroundings. Did you catch the time as you entered the Muppet Vision 3-D attraction? If not, don't worry, Gonzo did. Take

a look at the large clock at the entrance to the attraction and spot Gonzo hanging from the minute hand.

Note: In case you're wondering, he'll go around the clock face 8,760 times in the next year!

Secret in the Rain

Being Disney's Hollywood Studios, there are many tributes to classic films scattered about. Make your way behind Muppet Vision 3-D and you'll find a lamppost with an umbrella attached to it near a street curb at a corner. This tribute to the classic 1952 film, "Singing in the Rain," is a fun and interactive Walt Disney World secret few stop to enjoy, let alone even realize it exists. Grab a camera and have your subjects stand under the umbrella. . .and watch it begin to rain on them

while you take their picture! (Don't worry, they'll remain dry under the umbrella.)

GERTIE THE DINOSAUR

Located on the shore of Echo Lake is Dinosaur Gertie's Ice Cream of Extinction. More than just a nod to the Novelty Architecture of Los Angeles in the early 20th century, this towering dinosaur is Disney's homage to Winsor McCay, an American cartoonist who played a role in inspiring a young Walt Disney to become an animator. On February 18th, 1914, when Walt Disney was only 12 years old, Mr. McCay released an innovative silent cartoon titled "Gertie the Dinosaur", which is recognized as being the very first cartoon ever produced which featured an animated character.

MIN AND BILL'S

Found on the opposite shore of Echo Lake is the S.S. Down the Hatch, an old tramp steamer which houses Min and Bill's Dockside Diner. *Min and Bill* was the name of a 1930 movie starring Marie Dressler (Min) and Wallace Beery (Bill), and it told the story of the struggles of Min, the manager of a run down dockside inn who raises a young woman, Nancy, to be a lady amidst the seedy and rough life of the docks, all while tangling with Bill, a loveable yet cantankerous fisherman. The film was a nationwide hit, earning Marie Dressler an Academy Award for Best Actress and propelling both her and Wallace

Berry to stardom, with Berry eventually becoming MGM's highest paid actor in the early 1930s.

Flying high above Min and Bill's Dockside Diner is a set of International code flags and pennants, which borrows from a scene late in the movie. These are used as a means to communicate between ships, and in this case, they communicate a nautical advertisement for sea-going sailors. Alternating between letters (flags) and numbers (pennants), the message spelled out between the two masts reads...

DOCKSIDE DINER
782562896354

While the meaning of the message "Dockside Diner" is apparent, the number sequence 782562896354 is a bit of an ongoing mystery. Given Disney Imagineers rarely place story elements in the park with no meaning, there is likely a meaning behind these numbers. Perhaps they are the birthdates of the Imagineers who worked on the attraction? Research continues on this.

Note: The roman numerals "XXI" at the waterline of the stern reflects the draft of the ship. As you can see, the ship is sitting nearly 21' deep in the water. Photo courtesy of WDWGuidedTours.com

VALENTINE'S DAY, 1929

Continue around Echo Lake and make your way to The Great Movie Ride attraction. Study the 1930s era Dodge Touring Car in the gangster scene and you'll notice an old license plate affixed to the left front bumper. More than just random numbers, the digits 021 429 on the plate reflect the date of the Valentine's Day Massacre on February 14, 1929.

www.Disney-Secrets.com

THE HOLLYWOOD BROWN DERBY

The restaurant's name? It was coined in 1926 when Herbert K. Somborn opened what was initially a coffee shop in Los Angeles. At the time, the Governor of New York, Al Smith, was known for wearing his signature brown derby hat. He was in town when Herbert Somborn was choosing a name for his restaurant, so Herbert named it after the Governor's. . .brown derby.

Tip: Once you step inside, take a moment to look for a spotted Dalmatian. His coat hides a Hidden Mickey.

DINE WITH A DISNEY IMAGINEER

Any guest can enjoy a meal at The Hollywood Brown Derby, but did you know you can also share a meal with a real Disney Imagineer? You and up to nine other guests can reserve your own special meal in which you dine with a Disney Imagineer involved with a specific area of Walt Disney World Resort. Ask any question you'd like as you enjoy a four-course meal of contemporary American cuisine, all topped with amazing insights into the world of Disney Imagineering.

Dining with Disney Imagineers is available for lunch at The Hollywood Brown Derby and the Flying Fish Restaurant at Disney's Boardwalk Resort.

Tip: It is strongly recommended that you make reservations 180 days in advance. Call 407-WDW-DINE (407-939-3463) for additional information and to make those reservations.

www.Disney-Secrets.com

SUNSET BOULEVARD

Most guests to Disney's Hollywood Studios step right on top of this next secret and never realize it. Others stare right at it, but haven't a clue as to its significance.

On the street corners of Sunset

Boulevard, guests will find an imprint in the cement which reads, "Mortimer & Co. 1928 Contractors." This is an homage to Mortimer Mouse, the name Walt Disney originally considered for Mickey Mouse, and 1928 is a reference to the year in which Mickey Mouse was not only "born", but also made his debut in the animated cartoon "Steamboat Willie."

Note: The image you see here is an optical illusion for most viewers. While the letters appear raised, they're actually imprinted into the concrete so they won't wear away with all of the guest foot traffic. To view the image properly, think of the light source as coming from the lower left corner, instead of the upper right.

A TRIBUTE TO FLORA DISNEY?

This next secret is a bit of a mystery. It is a tribute, but to whom?

Located in the ticket booth of the Legends of Hollywood Theater on Sunset Blvd. is an antique paperweight. With a date of 1958 being clearly visible on the left of two medallions, the paperweight commemorates the 50th anniversary of New York's stately Singer Building, which was built in 1908 and, for a brief period, was the tallest building in the world. Measuring 4.5 inches long and 2.5 inches wide, the paperweight is made of bronze, and the handle itself is an exact replica of the small

bronze anchors which the window cleaners used when anchoring themselves to the exterior of the building.

Nothing in the parks is placed at random by the Imagineers, especially a piece such as this. The small sign on the General Store in Frontierland for A.C. Dietz Lanterns ties to Walt and the early days of Disneyland, the gas lamps of Main Street, U.S.A. are exact replicas of the very first gas street lamp ever used in America, and the colorful Mutoscopes of Town Square are an obscure tribute to Winsor McCay, whom is recognized by Disney as being a very important inspiration for Walt becoming an animator.

Initially, one might think this is an obvious tribute to Isaac Merritt Singer, the inventor of the Singer Sewing Machine, but he lived well before Walt's time and had no interactions with Walt. In addition, while the Singer Building was located in New York, it was not home to the offices of Charles Mintz, the man who stole Oswald the Lucky Rabbit from Walt, or Margaret Winkler, the woman who helped Walt a great deal. Both would make for a perfect tie in with the paperweight's placement in the theater, but they have no application here.

It turns out this paperweight may be a cleverly hidden tribute to Walt's mother, Flora. In 1906, Walt's parents, Elias and Flora, moved their family to Marceline, Missouri. Shortly after their arrival, Elias bought Flora a sewing machine, and given Singer sewing machines were by far the most popular model in use across the country at the time, it is safe to assume it was a Singer model. In my research involving the Walt Disney Hometown Museum, they indicated that Walt's sister, Ruth, had told the Museum's Director that Flora was an accomplished seamstress, making clothing for the entire family. In addition, she was also part of a rural farm organization that made quilts in the area.

But why is this tribute located in the Legends of Hollywood Theater? It's because Isaac Singer was at one time a theater manager in New York before going on to invent the Singer Sewing Machine Flora Disney would use to clothe Walt and the entire Disney family throughout the years, beginning in Marceline. Photo courtesy of WDWGuidedTours.com

ROCK 'N' ROLLERCOASTER STARRING AEROSMITH

Walk this way. . . .to the rotunda area of this attraction and take "note" of the busy pattern of irregularly shaped tiles in the colorful floor. Somewhere in that mix are two Hidden Mickeys. They are tiny, and it is a bit of a puzzle to find them, but it's a *sweet emotion* when you do. Each of the small Hidden Mickeys is made up of three small round circles, so they will stand out from the straight-edged tiles when discovered. You'd like a photo as a hint? Sorry, that'd be way too easy, and after all, it's a puzzle. Alright, time to get *back in the saddle again* to keep enjoying Disney's Hollywood Studios secrets.

Tip: If you think those are all the Hidden Mickeys, then...*dream on.* There are a few more in the Rock 'n' Roller Coaster Starring Aerosmith attraction, including an interesting-looking classic three-circle Hidden Mickey in the carpet, a coiled cable Hidden Mickey, three in the image of the band atop the limo, one that you "pick", and more.

BEAUTY AND THE BEAST
LIVE ON STAGE

If you opt not to see the Beauty and The Beast - Live on Stage performance, you will join the thousands who pass by this next secret each and every day unaware it exists. Make your way towards the entrance of the attraction and note all the famous celebrities who have left their handprints, as well as carved their names, in the cement.

THE TWILIGHT ZONE
TOWER OF TERROR

This next secret is an homage to a character in a classic episode of The Twilight Zone.

After entering the lobby of the Twilight Zone Tower of Terror, look for a pair of reading glasses sitting on the Concierge Desk. The glasses are a reference to the classic Twilight Zone episode "Time Enough at Last" in which Henry Bemis, (Portrayed by Burgess Meredith) a bookish man who loves to read, finds himself as the last man on earth after an atomic blast. He's thrilled to discover the ruins of a library packed with all kinds of fascinating books, and now, being all alone on the planet, he finally has all the time he wants to read them. The cruel irony of the Twilight Zone strikes, however, when to his horror he accidentally drops his glasses and breaks the lenses.

Now notice the poster behind the Concierge Desk which reads, "Anthony Fremont and His Orchestra". This is a reference to what is considered by many to be the best Twilight Zone episode ever produced. In this episode, titled "It's a Good Life", a young Anthony Fremont (Bill Mumy) is a six-year old boy who controls the world with god-like mental powers, but unfortunately wields them with the unlimited restraint and mind of a child, thus filling everyone in his town with fear. In addition to being able to control the weather, read minds, think objects into being and cast away people he doesn't like, young Anthony Fremont likes music, but he doesn't like singing, hence the musically themed poster.

The landscaping outside the Hollywood Tower Hotel isn't just random growth. It was designed specifically to mimic the hillsides found around the Elysian and Griffith Parks areas of Los Angeles as a means to lend more authenticity to this Hollywood area hotel.

The music playing? It's Glenn Miller's "Sleepy Time Gal" and Duke Ellington's "Mood Indigo", two songs which were popular at the time the Hollywood Tower Hotel was struck by lightning on October 31, 1939.

In a nod to the Disney Imagineers' attention to detail, within the lobby of the Tower of Terror is a copy of the Los Angeles Examiner newspaper dated on Halloween night, October 31, 1939. Fittingly, the cover story is about the capture of Ruth Judd, who escaped from prison where she had been sentenced for murder.

"Ruth Judd Gives Self Up After Six Days,
Returns to Asylum in Hysterics"

Note: This same newspaper appears at the Disneyland, Disney's Hollywood Studios and Disneyland Paris Tower of Terror attractions.

www.Disney-Secrets.com

KEEPING YOU IN STITCHES

Here's a secret which gives a personal touch to your own souvenir. Visit Adiran & Edith's Head to Toe at Disney's Hollywood Studios and, for a price of usually $10 or less, have any Disney-Parks purchased item, such as shirts, caps, mouse ears, t-shirts, etc. embroidered with your own custom name, phrase or favorite Disney character.

TWILIGHT ZONE HIDDEN MICKEY

The Twilight Zone Tower of Terror is home to a number of Hidden Mickeys. Guests watching the episode of the Twilight Zone, which introduces the attraction, will notice a stuffed Mickey Mouse doll being held by a little girl as she and her family board the elevator. In addition, as your elevator car reaches the "fifth dimension," pay special attention to the swirling stars and watch them quickly form the head of Mickey Mouse.

A Rerun for the First Time

Think you've seen that episode of The Twilight Zone before? Chances are you have...at least the initial portion of it. The Imagineers created this custom episode specifically for the attraction, and they  drew inspiration for it from the opening moments of a 1961 episode titled "It's a Good Life."

Tip: For a fun family photo when riding the Twilight Zone Tower of Terror, hold up your park map and act as if you're casually studying it just at the moment the elevator drops...and the camera flashes. While the photo captures those around you screaming in terror, you appear cool, calm and collected while searching the map for where to find a churro. Better yet, use a book for an even more casual look. Be sure to hold the map or book a bit low, or it will rise and obscure your face in the photo as the elevator drops!

SECRETS OF DISNEY'S ANIMAL KINGDOM

"Welcome to a kingdom of animals...real, ancient and imagined: a kingdom ruled by lions, dinosaurs and dragons: a kingdom of balance, harmony and survival; a kingdom we enter to share in the wonder, gaze at the beauty, thrill at the drama, and learn."

- Michael Eisner – Dedication of Disney's Animal Kingdom

AN EXCLUSIVE ENTRANCE

Next I reveal a secret side entrance to Disney's Animal Kingdom that will have you skirting long lines in the hot Florida sun.

During the high-season, crowds at the entrance to Disney's Animal Kingdom can be quite large, especially early in the day. While others wait in long lines at the main entrance, step over to the adjoining Rainforest Cafe and make your way towards the rear of the gift shop where you will find a separate out-of-the-way side entrance to Disney's Animal Kingdom.

AN INTERACTIVE HELLO

Upon arriving at the park first thing in the morning, most guests rush to enter the Oasis and quickly move on to their favorite attractions, and it is here they miss one of the first secrets of the day. Make it a point to arrive at Disney's Animal Kingdom early in the morning, and you will find Cast Members standing nearby who are holding small sociable animals for up close interaction with children and other guests.

THE OASIS

As with all Disney parks, guests are taken on a journey of transition from the outside world to a land of magic and wonder as they enter Disney's Animal Kingdom.

As you move through The Oasis, refrain from rushing further into the park and take a moment to notice how the Disney Imagineers purposely designed it to transition guests from the outside world to the world of wonder which awaits. Notice how enchanting music has begun to fill the air while winding paths, cool waterfalls, towering plants, and lush greenery all begin to transport guests to another land. Just as with emerging from the tunnels into the Town Square at the Magic Kingdom, guests emerge from The Oasis to a stage of exotic animals, stunning habitats, exciting thrills and engaging education.

Tip: If you take the time to slowly stroll through The Oasis and explore its different paths, foliage and waterfalls, you will discover the beautiful Macaws, each perched close to the trail.

A 30' HEIGHT LIMIT

As you walk past, in and around the buildings of Disney's Animal Kingdom, notice how they are often overshadowed by tall trees and objects. Disney Imagineers purposely limited the height of buildings in this park to 30 feet, thus capturing and conveying the dominating essence of the landscape.

THE TREE OF LIFE

Stop and pay attention to the leaves of The Tree of Life. Watch them for a while and you'll notice they're not static, but instead moving each time the wind blows. Note that because the Tree of Life is not real, it cannot grow leaves. As a result, the Imagineers had to affix each and every leaf on the tree, and to ensure it all looked realistic when finished, each leaf was designed to gently move in the breeze.

It's no secret that the Tree of Life is large. At 14-stories tall, it rises 145 feet high. Its bark is a tapestry of over 350 carved animals, and its 8,000 branch tips hold 103,000 leaves made up of five different shades of green.

A TRIBUTE TO JANE GOODALL

Near the entrance to "It's Tough to be a Bug", you'll find a touching tribute to Jane Goodall, a British primatologist who engaged in courageous ground-breaking research of primates in the wild as part of her 45-year study of their social interactions in Gombe Stream National Park, Tanzania. The tribute consists of a plaque and an impressive sculpture of David Greybeard, a grey-chinned male chimpanzee who was the first to accept Jane Goodall into his community. The sculpture provides an excellent opportunity to see the detailed work of the Tree of Life bark up close.

DISCOVERY ISLAND TRAILS

As you journey through the Discovery Island Trails near the Tree of Life, look for a rock with small holes in it. While at first glance it appears to be simply a part of the landscape, if you peer into the holes, you'll find each one highlights a specific animal on the Tree of Life.

CAN'T JOIN THE FOLD

Everyone loves a free souvenir. The Disney Imagineers discovered this in the early days of Disneyland, as it seems guests would sometimes take anything from the park that wasn't nailed down. With the 3-D glasses for It's Tough to be a Bug! being somewhat small and obviously "mobile", they had to come up with a way that would keep guests from taking them as a souvenir, otherwise they'd have to replace thousands of glasses each day. The trick?...they made them such that they cannot be folded, thus making them more difficult to stow or walk away with.

HARAMBE

In designing the village of Harambe, Disney Imagineers borrowed from the architectural elements found in the coastal town of Lamu in Kenya. Realizing the story reaches far beyond just the architecture, they incorporated the elements which make Harambe seem even more realistic, including the worn appearance of the town's buildings and structures, its cracked sidewalks, dusty pathways, distinctive signs, hectic noise and more.

A TRIBUTE TO JOE RHODE

If it's time to eat, then it's time for discovering a secret which is a nod to Joe Rhode, the Disney Imagineer who played the lead role in designing and developing Disney's Animal Kingdom. Step inside Tusker House Restaurant, make your way to the main buffet area and take note of the balcony on the second floor. There you will find a storefront for "Jorodi Masks & Beads". Now sound out "Jorodi" and "Joe Rhode". Do you hear the audio homage? Clever, isn't it? But it doesn't end there. Also attached to the balcony is a sign which reads "Earrings", which is also a nod to Mr. Rhode and the unique earring he is known for wearing in his left ear. Photo courtesy of DisneyBabiesBlog.com

TOW AWAY ZONE

While staying at the Hotel Burudika, you'll want to heed this sign in Swahili and leave your livestock somewhere else. Loosely translated, it means "No Permission to Install Livestock In Front Of This Wall".

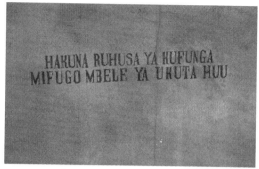

Did you notice the sign atop the entry to the railcar on the Wildlife Express? It also tells you that no livestock is allowed on the train.

SOUNDS LIKE HARAMBE

While much of the story at Disney's Animal Kingdom is told with visual elements, such as landscaping, architecture, color, perspectives and more, Disney Imagineers have also filled the park with creative sounds, each of which is designed to add to the story. From the distant...and purposely distinct...whistle of the Wildlife Express train to the roar of the Expedition Everest cars as they scream down the mountainside, sound fills the park and completes the magic. However, if guests don't pay attention, much of it will be missed, and that part of the story will remain untold.

Make your way to in front of the Tusker House in Harambe and listen for a while to hear sounds which have been added to help create a sense of the bustle of the small village. Pause and listen for the landlady who is banging on a door upstairs trying to get into a room.

Now continue this audio discovery by moving over to the nearby Tusker House Restaurant and listening closely to the sounds of a very busy kitchen emanating from somewhere close by.

Baloo is Hiding Around the Corner

Now make your way over to Tamu Tamu Refreshments to find an Imagineers' secret, which has been skillfully hidden in plain view right in front of guests. There, on a partial wall in the seating area behind the restaurant and near the path to Asia is a patchwork of plaster shaped to resemble Baloo, the bear from Disney's popular 1967 animated film, The Jungle Book.

Kilimanjaro Safaris

Kilimanjaro Safaris is an amazing adventure filled with all kinds of African animals, all of which appear in a natural habitat setting, and for many guests, animals such as the lions, elephants, cheetahs and crocodiles are the highlights of the attraction.

Here's what you need to know to get the best view of these magnificent animals. Like most attractions, seating is assigned by a Cast Member once you reach the ride vehicle. The lions, elephants, crocodiles and cheetahs are on the left side of the vehicle as you move through the attraction, so to get the best view during your journey, ask the Cast Member seating guests if you may be seated on the left side of the vehicle, in the back row. This gives you the very best view of all of these animals, and you'll get much better pictures, as well.

Note: The Hippos also tend to be seen on the left side of the vehicle, though not always. The stately giraffes are very mobile throughout the attraction and can be seen on either side.

Tip: Want to get a photo like the one above, with the ride vehicle making the turn while an elephant stands in the background? It takes two things to get it, one you can control, and the other is pure (mostly) luck. When you board the ride vehicle, ask to be seated on the far left side of the very back row. Now, as you make your way through the attraction, have your camera ready once you pass the large Baobab tree, where the elephants gather. Being located in the back seat, you'll have an unobstructed view of the scene after you pass the tree and won't have any other guests' heads in the foreground, as you would if you took this same picture from another seat in the ride vehicle. You'll still have to twist and contort quite a bit to get the shot, but it is worth it for this classic Kilimanjaro Safari photo. As far as the elephant in the background and the ride vehicle making the turn at just the right time?...well, that's the luck part, but the ride vehicles are evenly spaced during the trip, and there is often food left right at the spot in which the elephant is standing, so odds are in your favor.

Island Hidden Mickey

As the ride vehicle makes its way through the attraction, it passes a large Baobab tree, which is often frequented by elephants. Just beyond the tree is a large pond with a small island inhabited by flamingos. Look closely, and you'll see the shape of the island is actually a Hidden Mickey.

Tip: Visit Google Earth to see this Hidden Mickey in detail.

The Smallest Hidden Mickey In The World

Want to find one of the smallest Hidden Mickeys in all of Walt Disney World Resort? Then locate a merchandise cart near the exit of Kilimanjaro Safaris and search the tile on the counter. There, embedded in the grout, are three tiny beads in the  shape of a classic three-circle Hidden Mickey. There are those who will tell you this is the smallest Hidden Mickey in all of

 Walt Disney World Resort, but to my knowledge, that claim belongs to the tiny Hidden Mickey found on the shirt of the caricature of Steve Barrett, The Hidden Mickey Guy, which can be found on a booth divider panel in the End Zone Food Court in the All Star Sports Resort. Hint:

Look for Minnie playing hockey. Hidden Mickey photos courtesy of WDWGuidedTours.com.

Your Very Own
Hidden Mickey

Now make your way to the nearby Pangani Forest Exploration Trail to help save the planet and maybe an endangered classic Hidden Mickey.

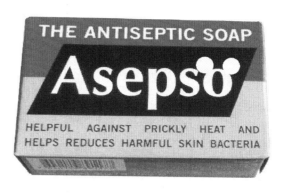

With the recent refurbishment of this attraction, the Research Station was renovated, and a number of items inside were removed, including the very popular Asepso soap box Hidden Mickey. One of the very first antiseptic soaps, Asepso became widely known overseas in the early 1900s as one of the first soaps to alleviate infections and reduce bacteria on the skin, but perhaps more importantly, it also cooled the skin and alleviated the effects of prickly heat in tropical climate locales, such as the Pangani Forest.

By using Asepso soap instead of a more generic American brand, Disney Imagineers had used a simple and very small prop to further immerse guests in the story that is the Pangani Forest Exploration Trail. And by adding two small circles to the front of the box, they created a whimsical...and classic...Hidden Mickey.

Unfortunately, this small box is now no longer part of the Research Station, no doubt because it would often go missing and, as a result, need frequent replacing. So how can we perhaps help bring about its return? By encouraging guests to make their own Asepso soap box Hidden Mickey souvenir! Simply go online to Amazon.com or another retailer and order a box, which may need to come from overseas. Once it arrives, apply a couple of round white stickers in a manner similar to the image above and you'll have your very own classic Disney's Animal Kingdom Hidden Mickey! Note that there are a number of different designs for the front of the box, some of which are similar but not the same as that which appears above.

HIDDEN MICKEY FLAP

While you're in the Research Station, find the backpack hanging on the wall and take note of the corner of the outer flap. Do you see the Hidden Mickey, next to the strap? Photo courtesy of WDWGuidedTours.com.

WILDLIFE EXPRESS TRAIN

The Wildlife Express Train is a narrow gauge train powered by a British steam engine, which as the *story* goes, was manufactured by Beyer, Peacock & Company in 1926. As you walk about Disney's Animal Kingdom, listen carefully to the distant sound of the train's steam whistle. Notice anything different about it? Unlike the more robust sound of the "American train whistles" at the

Magic Kingdom, the Imagineers made sure this whistle blasts with the higher shrill of a British steam engine, so as to ensure the accuracy of the story.

AN IDEA TRANSPORTED FROM DISNEYLAND

Now as you journey aboard the Wildlife Express Train, note that the seats are actually benches which all face the same way. Believe it or not, but this design ties back to a discovery made over 60 years ago, in the early days of Disneyland.

The first Disneyland Railroad cars were designed like any other in the country at that time. Guests would enter through the ends of the cars and walk down a center aisle with seats on each side, but disembarking from such a configuration takes a good deal of time and can be an exercise in frustration. In addition, it can keep the trains from running on time. Disney Imagineers soon realized that guests could more easily...and more quickly...board and disembark from the train if they could access the rail car from large openings on the side, instead of from a single doorway on each end. This design efficiency developed in Disneyland is now perfected today in the Wildlife Express Train 3,000 miles away!

OVER 100
HIDDEN MICKEYS IN ONE PLACE

Make the mistake of joining the multitudes who hurry past the entrance mural at the Conservation Station, and you'll pass up a delightful and engaging hour of fun for the whole family! As you enter the Conservation Station, stop to study the large mural on each side of the entrance hallway. Look closely, and you'll find countless Hidden Mickeys mixed in with the animal images. Do you see Mickey's face in the photo here?

In addition to being home to over 100 Hidden Mickeys, Conservation Station is an excellent opportunity for children of all ages to interact with small animals.

WILDLIFE EXPRESS
TRAIN STATION

The authentic architecture of the train station for the Wildlife Express Train reflects the elements typically found in the railroad stations of East Africa during the early 1900s.

A TRIBUTE TO BOB HARPUR

Disney Imagineers are honored all throughout Walt Disney World Resort, and if you look carefully at Engine 02594 of the Wildlife Express, you'll find the name of R. Baba Harpoor, a nod to Disney Imagineer Bob Harpur. Mr. Harpur not only shared an interest in miniature trains with Walt Disney, but he also played a key role in acquiring and restoring the locomotives in use at Walt Disney World Resort today.

www.Disney-Secrets.com

DiVine

Think all green leafy plants are the same? You may find out otherwise when you enter Disney's Animal Kingdom.

Unsuspecting guests walking between Africa and Asia are often surprised by DiVine, a tall walking plant on stilts which emerges from hiding in plain view amidst the foliage to delight guests, usually with a bit of surprise. Note that DiVine can be very difficult to spot, even though she may be right before your eyes. Standing on tall stilts and completely covered in ivy-like foliage, she may wrap herself around a tree, drape herself on a building or simply stand next to the trail, all while being perfectly camouflaged... until she starts moving.

Note: As with Disney characters, DiVine appears on occasion and only for a while, so she is not always in the park. In addition, she may appear in The Oasis at times.

DiVine photo courtesy of Aaron DelPrince

CHARGED FOR
A BOTTLE OF COKE

Here's a fun-to-discover secret the Disney Imagineers have placed as a creative story element, which guests just might find in a small Asian village. Just out from the entrance to the Kali River Rapids ride is a tall utility pole strung  with all kinds of wires, lights, insulators and more. Mixed in with that collection is an old Coke bottle, which, being made of glass, has been inverted and turned into an insulator.

KALI RIVER RAPIDS

 Ride interaction is a somewhat rare opportunity at Walt Disney World, but this next secret reveals a fun way to interact with guests on Kali River Rapids.

As you exit the attraction and make your way across the bridge which spans the Kali River, look for two small control panels placed on the right railing. These panels hold buttons which control the two ornately decorated elephants below, and pushing them causes a stream of water to squirt from the elephant's trunks onto unsuspecting guests in the rafts as they drift past.

EXPEDITION EVEREST

This next secret is an amazing display of the Imagineers' use of ride technology, which most guests miss because they are purposely distracted. As your train begins its harrowing journey high on the mountain, it careens around a corner before coming to a halt only a few feet away from a section of broken track hanging over a terrifying drop. Pausing for only a moment, it then begins to plummet backwards down the mountain and into the darkness before coming to a halt once again. Here's where you want to pay attention.

While the animated Yeti menace appears on a screen with a terrifying roar, look away and peer towards the opening straight ahead. There you will see an entire stretch of track "flip" over in preparation of sending you  screaming into the void and down the mountainside!

ABOUT THAT YETI

The fur on the fearsome yeti is a mix of yak fur, horse hair and synthetics, with a touch of Spanish moss thrown in.

According to the Disney Archives, the Yeti in Expedition Everest is the single most powerful Audio-Animatronic figure in use in Disney parks. The tallest?...That would be the Fantasmic dragon. And the smallest?...Chef Remy at the France pavilion in the World Showcase at Epcot.

DINOLAND, U.S.A.

Now step into Dinoland U.S.A. and find the Highway 498 sign located over by Primeval Whirl. Appearing to be simply a random design element, it actually ties in with three other "signs" scattered throughout all four parks, all of which denote the year the park opened. The Magic Kingdom opened in 1971, as indicated by Fire Station 71 in the Town Square, Epcot opened in 1982, as shown on the farmhouse mailbox of The Land, Disney's Hollywood Studios opened in 1989, as indicated on the gas  pumps of Oscar's Super Service gas station and Disney's Animal Kingdom opened on April 22, 1998, hence "Hwy 498."

AN ANCIENT HIDDEN MICKEY

Study the large murals you see as you enter the DINOSAUR attraction to find two ancient Hidden Mickeys. On your right as you enter, you'll find a mural with a tree on the left hand side. Study where a branch connects to the trunk  and you'll find a classic three-circle Hidden Mickey. Across the way, you'll notice a mural with the depiction of an explosion. Take a look amidst the chaos for another Hidden Mickey there.

IMAGINEERING WHIMSY

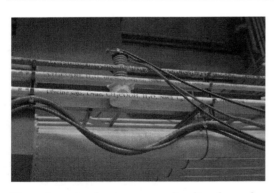 Disney Imagineers are a serious bunch, but they definitely have a whimsical side, as well. As you descend the stairs in the DINOSAUR ride vehicle staging area, notice the three pipes to the left colored red, yellow and white. The chemical compounds displayed on the pipes? They're for. . . ketchup, mustard and mayonnaise!

AMERICAN CROCODILE

The American Crocodiles of the Kilimanjaro Safaris attraction are impressive, but they are seen at a distance from the ride vehicle. This next secret reveals the whereabouts of an American Crocodile which is not only impressive in size, but also viewed from a much closer perspective. It is perhaps the closest you will ever come to a crocodile of this size, and unfortunately, most guests pass by without ever noticing it is there.

As you make your way towards Restaurantosaurus, stop and peer over the edge of the American Crocodile exhibit across from the restaurant. There, in the small pond, you will see a creature of gargantuan size only a few feet away. While often resting, keep an eye on it as it does periodically move.

Note: How real is the Discovery River at Disney's Animal Kingdom? So real that sometimes live alligators find their way into the river. Here is a photo I took of a young alligator swimming in the river between Asia and Africa.

Cretaceous Trail

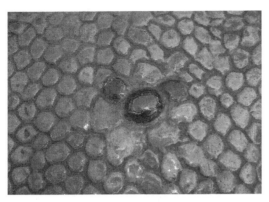

Hidden on the Cretaceous Trail is a classic Hidden Mickey just for kids. Don't walk past the large dinosaur on the ground without taking a close look at its back. Can you find the Hidden Mickey in its scales?

Thank You!

I hope you have enjoyed this journey through the secrets & stories of Walt Disney World as much as I've enjoyed sharing them with you. Remember, there are many more secrets which you'll walk past, over and through as you explore the dynamic and ever-changing magic of the parks. Where there is nothing today, there may be a new classic tomorrow just waiting to be revealed.

Go...discover the magic!

Mike Fox

THE HIDDEN SECRETS & STORIES OF DISNEYLAND

"Almost every page contained details I had never noticed before."

– Disney Legend Bob Gurr

If you enjoyed discovering the secrets of Walt Disney World, then you're sure to enjoy *The Hidden Secrets & Stories of Disneyland.* The companion book to this title, it is an entertaining and magical in-depth look at over 200 secret story elements hidden throughout Disneyland...all arranged as a fun tour, complete with photos!

Available online. Learn more at:

www.Disney-Secrets.com

ACKNOWLEDGMENTS

Many people have graciously contributed to the development of this book. From Michael Broggie's biography of his father and Disney Legend, Roger Broggie, and Jeff Baham's exclusive story about the attic scene in Disneyland's Haunted Mansion, to the Disney Archive's providing a key date for solving a puzzling timeline, and Dave Drumheller's big help in obtaining last-minute photos, many have played a role, large or small, in helping me write a title which contains not only quality content, but also family value entertainment which is respectful of the legacy of Walt Disney.

For that, I would like to thank you all...

- Beth Green – ADisneyMom'sThoughts.com
- Bob Gurr – Disney Legend and Imagineer
- Brian Hillman – George H. Lloyd Relative
- Brian Hull – Voice Impressionist/Singer/Composer
- Carrie Hayward – DisneyTravelBabble.com
- Chip Confer – ChipandCo.com
- Cindy Bothner – Walt Disney Imagineering
- Dave DeCaro – Davelandweb.com
- Dave Drumheller – WDWGuidedTours.com
- David Leaphart – SteelWheelonSteelRail.com
- David Lesjak – Disney Historian
- Disneyana Fan Club – Cascade Chapter
- Doobie Moseley – LaughingPlace.com
- Doug Leonard – Walt Disney Imagineering
- Frank Reifsnyder – Walt Disney Imagineering
- George Eldridge – Decoding the Disneyland Telegraph
- Glenn Barker – Walt Disney Imagineering
- Jack Ferencin – Hellertown, PA
- Jeff Baham – DoomBuggies.com
- Jeff Kober – PerformanceJourneys.com
- Jenn Lissak – DisneyBabiesBlog.com
- Jim Korkis – Disney Historian
- Jason Dziegielewski– DisneyGeek.com
- Jordan Sallis – George H. Lloyd Relative
- Michael & Sharon Broggie – Disney Historians
- Michael Campbell – President, Carolwood Pacific Historical Society

- Mike Ellis – MyDreamsofDisney.com
- Mike Westby – Disney App & Guidebook Author
- Mousestalgia.com Podcast
- Steve DeGaetano – Disneyland Railroad Historian – SteamPassages.com
- Tammy Benson – Golden Spike NHS
- The Disney Archives

And most of all my parents, Richard & Roberta, for taking me to Disneyland for the very first time many years ago!

Selected Bibliography

Many sources of content, including interviews, books, articles, documents, vintage publications, photos, correspondence, video and of course countless theme park visits were used in the research for this book.

Here are some publications which were not only helpful, but I would highly recommend them as reading material for anyone interested in Walt Disney World, Disneyland or Disney history...

Baham, Jeff. *The Unauthorized Story of Walt Disney's Haunted Mansion.* Theme Park Press, 2014

Bain, David Haward. *Empire Express: Building the First Transcontinental Railroad.* Penguin Books, 2000

Berg, Walter G. *Buildings and Structures of American Railroads.* 1893

Broggie, Michael. *Walt Disney's Railroad Story.* Donning Company Publishers, 4th Edition. 2014

DeGaetano, Steve. *The Disneyland Railroad – A Complete History in Words and Pictures.* 1st Edition. 2015

Gabler, Neal. *Walt Disney: The Triumph of the American Imagination.* Alfred A. Knopf, 2006

Kober, J. Jeff. *Disneyland at Work.* Performance Journeys, 2010

Kober, J. Jeff. *Disney's Hollywood Studios – From Show Biz to Your Biz.* Theme Park Press, 2014

Lloyd, George. *George H. Lloyd's Hand Carved Caenstone Model of Our National Capitol.* Lowenstein's, Approx. 1943

Sklar, Marty. *Dream It! Do It!: My Half-Century Creating Disney's Magic Kingdoms.* Disney Editions, 2013

Smith, Dave. *Disney A to Z: The Updated Official Encyclopedia.* Disney Editions, 1998

Strodder, Chris. *The Disneyland Encyclopedia.* Santa Monica Press, 2012

The Philadelphia Contributionship Digital Archives – Philadelphiabuildings.org

Thomas, Bob. *Walt Disney: An American Original.* Hyperion, 1994

Van Eaton, Mike. *Van Eaton Galleries Presents the story of Disneyland – an exhibition and sale catalog.* 2015

Wright, Alex and The Imagineers: *The Imagineering Field Guide to Disneyland.* Disney Editions, 2008

Wright, Alex and The Imagineers: *The Imagineering Field Guide to Epcot.* Disney Editions, 2006

Wright, Alex and The Imagineers. *The Imagineering Field Guide to The Magic Kingdom.* Disney Editions, 2005

www.Disney-Secrets.com

69742653R00098

Made in the USA
Columbia, SC
30 April 2017